DJ QUINN

Stick Figures: A Big Brother Remembers

A Memoir

AUTHOR
DJ Quinn

First published by DJQuinn 2023

Copyright © 2023 by DJ Quinn

All rights reserved. No part of this publication may be reproduced, stored or transmitted in any form or by any means, electronic, mechanical, photocopying, recording, scanning, or otherwise without written permission from the publisher. It is illegal to copy this book, post it to a website, or distribute it by any other means without permission.

Some names have been changed throughout this book for confidentiality.

Permissions

From CROSSING THE WATER: Eighteen Months on an Island Working With Troubled Boys-A Teacher's Memoir by Daniel Robb. Copyright © 2001 by Daniel E. Robb. Reprinted with the permission of Simon & Schuster, Inc. All rights reserved.

First edition

ISBN: 979-8-9893174-2-4

Cover art by Getcovers

This book was professionally typeset on Reedsy. Find out more at reedsy.com

*Dedicated to Elizabeth "Betty" Scott
She gave him a chance at life.*

Contents

I   Road to a Match

1	The First Figures	3
2	Here's A Kid For You	5
3	The Start Of The Journey	9
4	Meeting Betty	14
5	Match Day	17
6	Why Be A Big Brother?	22

II   Early Match

7	Calendars	29
8	Riding the Waves	33
9	'Twas The Week Before Christmas	36
10	A Morning Chat	40
11	Not Shicken—Chicken!	42
12	The Speedometer	46
13	Liar! Liar!	50
14	My Special Christmas Gift	56
15	The Sneak Attack	59
16	Showgirls!	63
17	Mike's Lucky Life	66

III Mid-Match

18	Story of a Sinking Ship	71
19	The Titanic: An Obsession	73
20	Escape From Children's Hospital	77
21	To Eat or Not to Eat	82
22	Random Wanderings	87
23	Gone Again	92
24	Reflections on the Run	96
25	… And Then God Sent Mike	100
26	The Little Green Group Home	106

IV Hospitals

27	The Visiting Hours	113
28	Wrestling Inside	118
29	Wedding Bells	123
30	Our Chess Stadiums	126
31	The Harry Potter Movie	130
32	Footsteps Approach	135
33	Sounding the Alarm	140
34	September 6, 2006	146
35	A Newspaper Sketch	149
36	The Chessboard	152
37	Bringing Mike Home	155
38	The Police Report	159

V Time Moves On

39	Betty's Passing	163
40	Bidding Goodbye	167
41	Epilogue	168

Acknowledgments 171
About the Author 173

I

Road to a Match

What can you do?
Get with a troubled young man, pay him attention;
convince him that he is sacred within;
help him see the Grendel who tramps through his veins;
help him see his parents for what they are -
flawed humans to be understood, forgiven, loved;
show him the possibility of seeing,
rather than standing in judgment;
teach him to laugh and love.
Expect to achieve none of this.
Do it anyway.

Daniel Robb, Crossing the Water

1

The First Figures

Without warning, my mind drifted into memory, into a space where imagination and reality frolic freely. I was immersed in a moment I had shared two years ago at the end of an outing with the kid.

The pen in my right hand moved slowly across the glossy paper. As he cuddled closer, his eyes followed each stroke to watch the picture inside the little box on the calendar page take shape. I could feel the dampness in his hair from our afternoon swim. He tried to disguise his snuggling as an excuse to see the page better, but I knew that this boy was a tactile kid who craved physical closeness.

Without a word, the crude shape of a swimming pool leapt off the page. The kid didn't realize that the tiny waves I added in the pool were the best of my artistic ability.

He edged closer, and I shifted the paper slightly. First, I added a small circle for a head, then a short vertical line that stopped just short of the pool deck. I lifted the pen and added two small legs to the bottom of the figure. Finally, a horizontal line crossed the body. The stick man was complete.

"This is you," I told him.

Then I repeated the process and drew a slightly taller stick figure with little bends in his legs. He was crouching slightly, prepared to jump into the pool.

"Tha—that one is you!" he exclaimed. "You gonna do a cannon-ball!" His words were choppy, his stutter worsening as he tired from our day's activities.

Two little stick figures. The two of us at the pool, crammed inside a small box that showed where today belonged when set on a page. Above them, the same two stick guys were pedaling bicycles past a crude drawing of Husky Stadium.

The figures were simple and drawn without adornments. Other than an occasional landmark sketched in the background, absolutely nothing cluttered their fun. Our stick figures never showed emotion, because when the boy and I looked at them we knew how they felt. Wherever they went and whatever they did, we knew they were happy just to be hanging out together.

Those sketches told a story. They illustrated the times the kid and I shared together as Big and Little Brother in the Big Brothers Big Sisters mentoring program. At the end of each outing, we sat on an overstuffed brown couch in his mom's living room. He snuggled closely, watching as I captured our day in a tiny stick figure sketch. When the drawing was finished, the boy would take his calendar and quietly examine the pages. What was going through his mind as he perused the collection of sketches?

Seeing him flip the calendar pages took me back further, back to a phone call I received before any of the stick figures came to be. That call launched our match as Big and Little Brothers.

What follows in these pages is my reflection on an extraordinary journey, a true story of times I shared with my "Little Brother" Michael Scott.

2

Here's A Kid For You

November 1992

I recognized her voice before she told me who was calling.
"This is Pauline from Big Brothers. Do you have a few minutes to talk?"

"Sure," I responded. "What's up?"

"I have a potential Little Brother that I think will work for you," she said. "I want to tell you about him and see if this sounds like a match that might work."

I was eager to hear what type of kid they had in mind. It had been three months since I submitted my application to Big Brothers of King County. It was the local chapter of the nation-wide Big Brothers organization, a non-profit that worked to match kids with a one-on-one mentor. At the time, the agency was looking for mentors to match with boys who did not have consistent adult male contact, primarily those living in a single parent home. Finally, after six hours of interviews, a police background check, and checking my references, I had been accepted to become a Big Brother. It would be my second time as a "Big," having volunteered for four years while living in Minnesota.

"His name is Michael, and he lives with his guardian in Seattle's Queen Anne area. He is seven years old and has been in and out of foster care since he was two. His guardian is named Betty, and she is in the process of formally adopting him. The adoption should be completed in a month or so."

"Betty is sixty-three years old," Pauline continued. "She is divorced and has three adult children of her own. Her daughter Linda lives nearby and helps her with Michael's care. One of Betty's sons is gay, and she is open to having a gay man as Michael's Big Brother."

So far, it sounded good.

"Michael was born with neurological problems and the most noticeable effects are in his speech. He has a condition called apraxia of speech, or verbal dyspraxia."

"I've never heard of it."

"Dyspraxia is like a short circuit along the neurological path. Michael has a difficult time verbalizing what he is thinking. He did not start talking until he was four years old. He goes to public schools, is in special education classes, and he works with a speech therapist."

A flash of seven-year-old me sitting with a speech therapist popped into my head. I was holding a paper, saying some special sentences she suggested structured so "S" sounds subtly slam a shy second grader who's struggling to slowly hiss S...,S...,S...." Pauline's voice was blocked out by the twinge of embarrassment and shame I felt—thirty years later—about having to go to speech therapy.

"Dennis?"

"Yes? Oh, sorry Pauline. Something distracted me." The speech therapist and young Dennis vanished.

"Okay. As I was saying, Michael's biological mother still lives in this area, but he doesn't have contact with her. He was returned to her on a couple of occasions after he was put into foster care, but always ended up being taken out of her home. Betty became his guardian because she was concerned that Michael was going to end up lost in the system."

"His biological mother was mentally ill, possibly suffering from schizophrenia. She had four daughters. All of them were removed from her home before Michael was born, and none are living in the Seattle area. Michael remembers his mother, but he doesn't know she had other children."

"What about his dad? Is he around?"

"There has not been any contact with his father, who was not the father of her other children. He is a Native man and apparently lives in British Columbia."

"Although Betty is not Native American, she has tried to expose Michael to his Native roots," Pauline continued. "She would like that to continue as part of his upbringing. Michael currently works with a counselor who is a Native American."

My mental picture of the kid was getting clearer. It was also getting very complex. On the other end of the phone call, pages flipped in the background, then Pauline continued.

"As far as activities go, Michael likes to do anything a seven-year-old would. He especially loves water. He takes swimming lessons, and Betty has him on a local swim team."

"When looking at what Betty would like to see in a match, she wants a Big Brother willing to help Michael learn boundaries. Emotionally, he is young for his age."

"What type of boundaries?" I asked.

"Social boundaries. For example, when he meets people, Michael immediately hugs them. He needs help learning when that is an appropriate behavior and when it is not."

"I see."

"There are also indications Michael suffered abuse while he was living with his biological mother." She paused momentarily and more papers shuffled on her end of the line. "That's a run-down on Michael. Do you have any questions, and does it sound like a match that might work?"

"There is one thing," I answered. "You mentioned abuse?"

"Yes, apparently there was some abuse in his background. It is unclear exactly what it was or how it affected him. But from what Betty has told us, he was abused."

"He sounds like a Little Brother I can work with. And since I was a Big Brother before, I am willing to take a kid that might be difficult to match. But I want to be clear about the abuse thing," I emphasized. "I do not want to step into something where a kid accuses me of something that isn't happening. I don't want to get in a situation where one day the child gets mad and decides to accuse me of hurting him. Do you understand?"

"Yes," she answered. "That is a legitimate concern. I have a sense from my talks with both Betty and Michael that, in this case, it is something we can work with. I will also make your concerns clear to Betty."

"Okay." I had made up my mind but didn't want to sound over-excited. "I'd like to give it a go."

"Great!" Pauline exclaimed. "I think you two will be a good match."

"So, what's next?"

"The next step is for me to contact Betty and tell her about you. If she wants to move forward, I'll set up a meeting for the three of us. If that meeting goes well and both of you are comfortable with the match, we schedule a match meeting with Michael."

"That sounds good."

"I do need to remind you," she stressed, "that the mom has the final yes or no on whether any match will be made."

"Sure, I understand. Thanks. I appreciate you calling."

When I hung up the phone, my hands were shaking.

"Hey! I hollered to Joe who was working downstairs. "I just got a new Little Brother!" This decision had taken so much time and effort. It was great to celebrate the moment with Joe, my long-term partner and best friend.

3

The Start Of The Journey

Joe and I met in the back of a DC-10 while working as flight attendants. It was the early 1980s, and we were both based in Minneapolis, Minnesota. He was the youngest of four siblings born and raised in Tampa, Florida. I hailed from Helena, Montana, the second oldest in a family of nine kids.

A great-looking, athletic guy who was wonderful with people, Joe had a super personality. He had a spirit that was a mix of old soul and wild child. With his fantastic sense of humor, he took things in stride and didn't get flustered by life's little annoyances.

From the very start, I loved him. He was friendly, energetic, and genuine. Joe was a man I could trust, a guy who was confident, a friend and partner who was patient with me. Our friendship turned into a romantic relationship in 1983, followed by marriage in 2013. He is the love of my life.

Pauline's description of my potential Little Brother was exciting. It sounded like working with him might be a challenging yet rewarding experience. The call was also heartening considering how badly the journey to this point had started several months earlier.

****

"We are looking for heterosexual role models for our kids."

I looked at the man standing in front of the room near the video screen. If I didn't know he was here to recruit volunteers for a non-profit, I would have pegged him as a used car salesman. He was clean-cut, middle aged, wearing a shirt, tie, and brown sports coat. The defining element of his appearance was the bored look on his face. His expression told the world his workday had gone on way too long.

Maybe I heard him wrong, but if he said that, then he'd made a mistake. *Heterosexual role models for our kids.*

I knew the guy was all wrong. I had been through this drill a decade earlier in Minneapolis. Forever etched in my memory was a conversation in 1980 with the case-worker during that volunteer screening for Big Brothers.

"I have to ask you about this," she said meekly. "What is your sexual orientation?"

"I am straight," I lied.

"Okay, thank you." She exhaled deeply. "Don't take it personally. It's a question we are required to ask all applicants. If a man is gay, it does not disqualify him, but the mother is told of a prospective volunteer's sexual orientation. The mom has the final say on whether or not to match the applicant with her son."

By the time I walked into the Seattle Big Brother orientation in 1991, things had changed for me. I had come out as a gay man to my family and closest friends. The process involved a lot of soul-searching, plenty of therapy, and many difficult conversations. I had taken big steps in accepting my sexual orientation and found huge relief from living honestly. There was no way I was going to lie and start walking backward into the closet.

The bored presenter showed a video followed by a quick run-through of the application process. He encouraged the men in the room to take an application home, complete it, and return the form as soon as possible. "We have around 270 boys on our waiting list," he said. "We are working hard to find heterosexual role models to help."

"Heterosexual role models." He said it again.

After the meeting, I approached him.

"Excuse me, you mentioned looking for 'heterosexual role models.'"

"Yep."

"Well, what's the policy on gay Big Brothers?"

"We don't take them," he replied flatly.

THE START OF THE JOURNEY

"What?"

"We don't take them."

"Uh, I thought Big Brothers left that issue up to the Little Brother's mom?"

"That's the policy of the national organization. King County is one of about five Big Brother agencies that doesn't do that. We don't take gay applicants."

"Why?"

"We had a lawsuit a few years ago. A mother of a Little Brother sued the agency. After that, our Board decided we would not take any gay applicants. The lawyers don't want the risk."

"So you have no gay Big Brothers?"

"Actually, there are a few matches that—" He hesitated. "There were some matches that were already in place, um, before ah, before the policy changed."

He was tripping on his words.

"And then, after it changed, well nobody said much, and since they were going before—."

He stopped suddenly, refocused, then shrugged.

"No. We do not accept gay Big Brothers."

"But I was a Big Brother before. For four years. Can't I even be considered?"

"Sorry." He started packing up his briefcase. This chat was getting me nowhere.

"Is there someone else I can talk with?"

"Call the executive director. Talk to him."

He snapped his briefcase and pointed toward the door. He walked right behind me, flipping off the lights.

Heterosexual role models. What the hell???

****

Later that week, I met with Chris Breen, executive director of Big Brothers of King County. He confirmed that what I heard in the orientation meeting was correct, that the policy was handed down from their Board.

"I appreciate your thoughts, Dennis," he explained. "Where we are now, my hands are tied. It will take a Board decision to change it, and there's been no indication they intend to do that."

Nothing I could say was going to change the situation. I sat there and glared at him.

"I know that other Big Brother agencies in the area, Tacoma and Snohomish County, do follow the national policy if you wanted to apply there," he offered.

"I am not going to be driving back and forth to Tacoma to be a Big Brother," I hissed. "Not when there are hundreds of kids waiting in Seattle, lots of them shut out by this policy."

It was a kick in the gut. Just as I was finally making progress opening up about my sexual orientation—WHAM! An organization that I'd had a successful run with before was not willing to consider me as a volunteer.

It wasn't about qualifications, references, or experience. They had 270 boys waiting to get a Big Brother. Most would never get one because there weren't enough volunteers. None of that mattered.

Right in the middle of liberal-leaning Seattle, one of the nation's best-known mentoring organizations was excluding qualified men from applying. Big Brothers of King County was not helping those kids on the waiting list by just "looking for heterosexual role models."

When I got home after meeting with Chris Breen, I wrote a letter expressing my thoughts. Their "heterosexual role models" policy was misguided. It contributed to the shortage of Big Brothers and wasn't an effective way to reduce the risk of abuse. I encouraged the Board to adhere to the same policy that their national organization and nearly every other Big Brother chapter followed.

****

Several months later the phone rang while Joe and I were watching a football game. Expecting a telemarketer, I was surprised when it was Chris Breen.

"Dennis, I appreciated your letter after our meeting a few months ago. I wanted to let you know I was able to take your letter and others like it to our Board," he said. "As a result, we have decided to change our volunteer application policy in line with the national organization, and we will accept applications from gay volunteers."

"I am glad to hear that," I replied. "Thanks for letting me know, and for your effort to get that changed."

"You are welcome. I wanted to let you know in case you would still like to be a Big Brother."

"I will be in to apply."

"Who was that?" Joe asked when I hung up.

"Big Brothers. They changed their policy. They are accepting gay volunteers."

It was rewarding to receive that call, hearing that my efforts had helped open the door for more volunteers. It would also increase the odds for more boys still waiting for a Big Brother to be matched, and made it possible for me to volunteer again.

Three months after receiving that call from Chris Breen, Joe and I took advantage of the policy change when we walked into the Seattle Big Brothers office together. We both submitted our volunteer applications.

4

Meeting Betty

She was waiting in the caseworker's office when I arrived. It was early afternoon and I was excited to meet the foster mother of my potential Little Brother.

"Hi, I'm Dennis," I said, extending my hand. "It's nice to meet you."

"And I'm Betty. I'm glad to meet you too."

Her long gray hair was parted down the center and pulled back in a ponytail. She was wearing blue jeans, a sweatshirt and tennis shoes, no makeup or jewelry.

That surprised me. I expected her to be more dressed up, the way my mother would be if she was out in public. Yet Betty was simply herself, comfortable, relaxed, and smiling.

"I'm glad you were both able to make it today," Pauline said. As soon as I sat down, she got right down to business.

"We like to use this time for you to get to know each other. We want to talk about the expectations you have if we all decide to go forward with this match. Then we'll talk about what might work well for Michael as a Little Brother."

"I've told each of you a bit about one another over the phone," Pauline continued. "Are there any questions either of you have since that conversation?"

Neither Betty nor I had questions that jumped right out. Pauline asked Betty to talk a bit about Michael and what things he liked to do.

"He is on the swim team, and he loves the water," Betty offered. "He would swim all day if he could. He doesn't like going to the mall. I took him there the other day and he hated it."

"How about going to football or basketball games?" I asked.

"He hasn't had the chance to do those things. I'm sure he would probably enjoy it, though. He likes to do new things, and I'd like him to have a chance to have a variety of experiences."

"Physical activity is good too," Betty continued. "It might help him a bit with his coordination. He's a hands-on kind of boy, he seems to learn from touching things. I also try to keep him involved with his Native heritage. He has a Native counselor, and he went to a Pow Wow a few weeks ago."

"Does he read yet?"

"No. He didn't start talking until he was four years old. He's in special education. Right now, they are working on learning letters and numbers. They also work with him on his speech, which is a big challenge."

Our conversation was a lot of chitchat, taking place under the ever-watchful eyes of Pauline. Obviously, the meeting was designed to let her have a chance to see how Betty and I interacted.

"Another thing we haven't talked about is how money will be handled on outings," Pauline chimed in. "Our goal is to have the match be built on one-to-one mentoring and friendship arrangements. What we want to avoid is developing a situation where the Little sees the Big as a guy who buys him things or who spends a lot of money on him. We all know that kids can be good at doing that."

Betty said she would cover Mike's expenses on outings. We both agreed it was something we would work on together. The meeting helped me relax and boosted my confidence about becoming a Big Brother for a second time.

The time we shared also helped me see that there was something special about Betty. She was unpretentious and genuine. I sensed she was at peace with herself, a gentle soul comfortably wrapped in the casual clothing she was wearing. She was easy to talk to and was someone I could easily work with.

"Now that we have met," Pauline said, "the next step is for both of you to think over what we talked about. Take a couple days, and let me know if any questions come up. Then, if you both choose to move forward, we will schedule a match meeting with Michael. Is there anything else you want to discuss today?"

Neither of us had any other questions, and we closed the meeting and exchanged pleasantries.

As I stood up to leave, Betty looked right at me and smiled. There was peace in her blue eyes.

"I've been praying for a miracle," she said. "And now here you are, standing right in front of me."

That was, without a doubt, one of the nicest things anyone had ever said to me.

5

Match Day

December 17, 1992

On the afternoon of my thirty-sixth birthday, I stepped out of my truck with a bad case of nerves. Less than half a city block, three concrete steps, and a quick knock on the front door were all that stood between me and a potential birthday gift. I was going to meet a seven-year-old named Michael, the kid who might be my new Little Brother.

Relax. I'm thirty-six years old. All I'm doing is meeting a little kid, right?

What made me nervous was knowing that once that door opened, the kid might become a part of my life. The four years I previously spent being a Big Brother in Minnesota taught me that once I was matched with a Little Brother, our paths would intertwine for a long, long time.

Since the day Pauline called, I had been forming a mental image of Michael created from her description. Now here I was, standing in front of a 1950s-style home with green shake siding. Beyond the silver chain link gate, a short sidewalk and three steps led to the door.

As nervous as I was, I had hauled along enough ego to give me just a slight edge of cockiness. Given time, I was sure I would be able to help this kid. At the top of the steps, my fear had a momentary stare-down with the storm door. There was no turning back. With the small gift I brought for Michael tucked under my left arm, my right hand made a fateful move, four firm knocks that rattled the storm door.

Muffled footsteps approached the door, the knob started turning. Yanking motions from the other side jostled the doorknob, and then suddenly a strong jerk pulled the door open. The suction from the opening door pulled the storm door tightly closed.

The roly-poly kid inside looked at me briefly, then focused his gaze on the storm door handle. Reaching up with both hands, he tried unsuccessfully to open the latch. Just as I reached out to help open it, he took a step back. He raised both arms and charged. Seventy-two pounds of unbridled energy bulldozed the door open and nearly sent me flying backward down the stairs.

"Michael? Hi, I'm Dennis, your Big Brother."

He stared at me with dark brown eyes from a face that looked more Asian than Native American. He uttered some garbled response I couldn't decipher. Then he lunged forward, locked a tight bear hug around my waist, and rested his head sideways on my hip. An uncontrolled thought shouted out inside my head. *How handicapped is this kid?*

Immediately the familiar gut punch of Catholic guilt hit me. That uncontrolled thought felt so brutal. How could my first reaction to meeting my Little Brother be: *How handicapped is this kid?* Talk about judgmental!

"Come on!" he said. I followed him through a set of brown French doors into a sitting room filled with toys. Michael's movements inside the house mirrored his door-opening technique. Neatly dressed in a red-and-white striped shirt, blue jeans and tennis shoes with Velcro straps, he had all the grace of a wild bull. Despite the chaos his movement stirred up, I sensed a sweet gentleness in his spirit.

Betty and Pauline were seated in easy chairs, intensely watching the interaction between Michael and me. Pauline was sharply dressed in a dark skirt and print blouse, surrounded by her ever-present aura of controlled seriousness.

Betty looked exactly as she did when I first met her, wearing blue jeans, plain tennis shoes, a tan sweatshirt, her gray hair pulled back in a ponytail. Her long face was accented by a set of simple wire-frame eyeglasses. A sense of no-nonsense also flowed from Betty that day, but still she was friendly to me. She seemed free of pretense or any concern what others might think.

"Si . . . Si . . .Sit down," Michael said, pointing to the couch.

As soon as I did, he crashed down next to me and snuggled up close. His mouth hung open slightly as he stared me up and down. His gaze chased my cockiness away, triggering the nerves I had hoped to leave on the doorstep. *I hope he likes me.*

The formalities of the match meeting started with Pauline reviewing all the rules with Betty, Michael, and me. The entire time she talked, the kid continued to size me up.

I was too distracted to concentrate on the rules. Meeting Michael had sparked a hope inside that I might be able to do some good for him. It was easy to see that the bundle of energy snuggled beside me had an impressive package of challenges. Whatever they were, they were wrapped inside a very happy spirit. I liked Mike and sensed that spending time with him was going to be unique.

As Pauline continued reciting the litany of rules, Betty's eyes met mine from across the room. We both smiled. She had already earned a special place in my heart. I admired her willingness to take Michael into her care, first as a foster parent and soon to become his adoptive mom. She was unselfishly giving him a chance at life, and he was very lucky to have this wonderful woman as his new mom.

Long before Pauline finished the formalities, his eyes were glued to the small package I had set on the coffee table.

"Here, Michael," I said, handing him the gift.

A smile lit up his face, then dissolved into an intent gaze as he tried to unfasten the tape on the package. When he couldn't, he grabbed the wrapping paper with both hands, and threw his elbows back with full force. The calendar inside flew to the floor, leaving Michael holding two handfuls of wrapping paper.

"This is for you," I said as I picked up the calendar and handed it to him. "It's to keep track of the days we will get together." I pointed to where "Match Day" was written on December 17.

"Oh." He roughly flipped through the pages, noticing where holidays were marked on the various months. His rough gross motor skills were putting the calendar in danger of being torn to shreds.

"See here," I said as I took the calendar, "this is October. Do you know what this says, here on October 5?"

"No."

"It says 'Michael's birthday.'"

He grinned and started flapping his arms up and down like a bird.

"My birf-day!"

"What do you say, Michael?" Betty asked.

"Th-tank you! Tank you!"

After a quick discussion with Betty, we set a date for our first outing, in five days.

"Hey, Michael," I suggested, "if you get me a pencil, we'll put that in the calendar."

Mike shuffled into another room and returned with a pencil. He watched closely as I wrote 'Mike & Dennis' in the box for December 22.

"We are here today." Together Mike and I counted the five boxes to the marked one on the 22nd. "And here is when we will get together. Okay?"

His arms flapped excitedly. Then he grabbed the calendar and stared at the words.

"Tank you!"

"You are welcome. I am glad you are going to be my Little Brother."

"Me too!"

He followed me to the door, then charged in and gave me another bear hug around my waist.

"Hey, Michael, let me show you something."

He let go and looked up.

"This is a special handshake we get to use. Hold out your hand like this." I extended my right hand; he followed my example.

"Okay, put your thumb between my thumb and my first finger. Then I put mine between your thumb and your first finger. Then we close the other fingers and we shake hands. This will be our special Big Brother and Little Brother handshake, just for us. Okay?"

He nodded and released my hand. Then he stood there just staring at his

MATCH DAY

own hand for several seconds.

"Bye, Michael. I will see you in a few days."

I closed the storm door and walked down the steps. When I turned to latch the gate, I saw Mike looking out the door smiling, flapping his arms again to say goodbye.

6

Why Be A Big Brother?

Small drops of water fell from the canopy of cedar branches overhead as I walked the dirt trail. All day the precipitation had been light and erratic, falling as rain before turning to snow, then stopping briefly only to return as rain.

Parts of the path were dimly lit from nearby streetlights. The hush of the night was interrupted by the whooshing sound of water spraying from the tires of cars passing on nearby Aurora Avenue. Inside the cocoon of privacy this trail through Woodland Park offered, I started to cry.

Three hours ago, Michael opened the door to his home, gave me a quick smile, and then wrapped a bear hug around my waist. In that moment, I knew my life had changed. Now, walking alone in the rain, I couldn't stop crying. I was drowning in gratitude for being given my new "Little Brother." When Michael opened that door, a powerful realization hit me. Deep inside I knew it was an important juncture in Michael's life. And in mine.

When I left, Michael gave me a hand-made Christmas ornament. It was a round metal cap with his school photo, a smiling seven-year-old in a red shirt with a content look in his dark brown eyes. I hung it on my Christmas tree when I got home, then called my parents to touch base and let them know I was thinking of them.

Then I headed out to walk. As I strolled on the path, a random thought flashed in my mind. *Someday I will write a book about my time with this boy.*

WHY BE A BIG BROTHER?

****

Why did I want to become a Big Brother? My motivation has often been questioned. It wasn't that deep. The source was television commercials.

Growing up in a family of nine kids, TV commercials served three primary purposes. First, a commercial break was the starting gun for the perpetual race to get into the bathroom. Second, the program breaks were small bits of time we used to wash, dry, and put away dinner dishes in frantic spurts. And finally, commercials fueled never-ending arguments over the seating arrangements in front of the small color TV our family shared. Any kid who left their spot without calling "place back" lost their seat to another, who then refused to move when the program restarted.

At some point during the chaos, public service announcements asking guys to volunteer as Big Brothers caught my attention.

"Just spend some time with a child," a pleasant voice would say over the arguments about seating arrangements. "A couple hours a week—that's all it takes."

I never knew anyone who had been a Big Brother. Or a Little Brother, for that matter. All I knew was what I heard on those commercials. To me, the concept of kids growing up without their dad around was foreign. It was also unsettling. Both my parents were actively involved in our family's daily life. My siblings and I spent our lives having each other as built-in best friends, a life that was anchored by the steady presence of our parents. Those Big Brother commercials made me feel sorry for any kid growing up without their dad around.

"If I ever move away from home," I told my sister Peggy one day, "maybe I'll be a Big Brother."

How hard could it be? Just hang around with some kid who doesn't have a dad. Go to the movies. Take him to some ballgames. Maybe just let him tag along now and then. It didn't sound too challenging.

****

When I moved to Minneapolis after college, it was my first time living away from my family. My flight attendant job had erratic schedules and offered more free time than I was used to. So I decided to apply as a Big

Brother volunteer and help some kid. In March 1980 I was matched with my first "Little Brother," an eleven-year-old named Scott. When we met, I had no idea how my time and experiences with Scott would affect me.

Being matched with Scott gave me a friend and opened my eyes to a life much different from mine. I grew up in a house surrounded by eight siblings and my parents; Scott grew up as an only child with his mom in an apartment. When I was a kid, I saved my earnings from my paper route to upgrade my bicycle; Scott used his paper route money to help his mom pay the rent. Whenever I came home from school, my mom and several brothers and sisters were there; Scott came home from school to hang out alone until his mom arrived from work hours later.

Four years spent as Scott's Big Brother helped me step out of my comfort zone. That commitment as a Big Brother also proved to be an anchor of stability. It tempered continual temptations to change my living arrangements, job assignments, or base locations during the turbulence of adjusting to life after college.

My time with Scott also taught me that becoming a Big Brother wasn't a step to take lightly. It was a commitment, it required being reliable to someone else. What started over a pizza in Burnsville, Minnesota, evolved through countless movies, ballgames, bike rides, and scaring the hell out of him when he was home alone one Halloween, into a wonderful friendship. I taught him how to drive and snow ski. He taught me that being his Big Brother didn't mean I could change his environment, his family, or their financial situation. What our match did was give us the chance to learn from each other, share time together, and to expand our horizons.

When I decided to move from Minnesota to Seattle in 1984, it was a choice that deeply affected Scott. One of the toughest parts of that move was telling my Little Brother I was leaving him.

Scott and I are still in touch today. I was his best man when he married his wife, Tammy, and he gave me the honor of being his son Mike's godfather. Scott is a wonderful man and remains a great friend. He has shown me time and time again that he has become exactly what I hoped my Little Brother would become: a compassionate, giving, and loving father, grandfather, husband, and friend. My relationship with Scott showed me that Michael and I could be at the start of something very significant for us.

Knocking on the door of Michael's home that afternoon was a commitment to accept him as he was, and a commitment to do what I could to help him. This time around as a Big Brother, I knew I wasn't there to change him. My job was simply to show up, be patient, and try to enjoy our time together no matter where this journey might take us.

II

Early Match

*The rules to the game are very simple:
Whoever has the most fun wins.*

7

Calendars

"Mike, why don't you get your calendar?" Betty asked. He stood up from his seat next to me on the couch, shuffled into the dining room and pulled out his calendar from a small drawer. Whenever we returned from an outing, we sat in the living room and spent some time chatting with Betty about that day's adventures. Then Mike fetched the calendar, returned to the couch, and plopped down next to me. Without a word he would hand me a pen and the calendar.

The simple gift I gave him the day we were matched had grown to serve a dual purpose. The calendar was a visual way for Mike to keep track of our next scheduled outing; the stick figure drawings we added at the end of our adventures evolved into a simple history of our times together.

Our initial Big Brother / Little Brother outings were easy-going bits of time together, intended to help us get to know each other and see what activities worked. Our first adventure was walking to a park near his home to play basketball. As uncoordinated as I had been from the day I was born, playing basketball with Mike made me feel like Michael Jordan. As soon as we stepped on the court it was evident that basketball essentials like dribbling, shooting, passing, and catching the ball were far beyond Mike's abilities. Using both hands, he would wind up his body and fling the ball, only to have it land two feet away. He discovered kicking the basketball was a much easier way to move it across the court. Mike's shooting mechanics were a two-handed heave straight up, sending the ball three feet over his head before it landed somewhere behind him.

The final play of our first (and only) basketball game was a pass I made to Mike. He held both hands up to catch the ball, but it zipped between his hands and smashed him in the face. Game over. We walked home, Mike crying and me apologizing profusely. The end of that first outing was never recorded with stick figures because I was too busy explaining to Betty how I clobbered her kid with a basketball.

Obviously, we had to keep athletics completely out of our adventures, so Mike and I went to see *The Lion King* movie with Joe, Nate, my sister Mazie, and her six-year-old son Vince. Mike was fixated on the screen during the whole movie, a big smile on his face. I remember looking over at him as the song *"Circle of Life"* was playing, and wondering where his life's path might take him. The film was a success, and the movie clearly beat basketball by a country mile.

As our relationship continued to develop, the dynamics of our outings shifted. Mike and I arrived at a point where we needed to establish a few boundaries. One afternoon the two of us headed to Marymoor Park, a 640-acre recreation area in Redmond, just east of Seattle. With trails, water, and a playground, it was a superb place to hang out for a couple hours. When we were walking toward the play area, Mike decided he had other plans. He turned around and walked in the other direction.

"Hey, Mike, we're going this way," I said.

"No. I want to go there." He pointed toward the creek, a spot where I knew he would immediately turn into a wet, muddy mess.

"Let's go play first. We'll stop there later."

He glanced at me but continued walking away.

"Mike, we are going this way first. Come on."

This time, Mike turned around and stared. Then he bent over, scooped up a handful of gravel and threw it at me.

"That's enough, Mike!"

He reached down again, grabbed more gravel, and pitched it my direction. The rocks landed several feet away from me.

"Okay, that's enough. Get into the truck. We are going home."

"Huh? We what?" he asked.

"We are going home. We're through for today."

"It's not-not time."

"We are done. Get in the truck."

I walked to the truck; Mike stood there, glaring. Finally, he moved toward the vehicle, kicking gravel the entire way.

"Why do we leave? It's not time," he shouted, slamming his door.

"We don't throw rocks at each other, Mike. That's not how Big Brothers works. So I'm taking you home."

The silence on the ride back to Betty's was unbroken. I didn't want to come down too hard on Mike, but I needed to make sure he got the message. Betty was out running errands when we arrived home, so Mike and I waited on her porch. She was stunned to find us sitting there an hour early, but she understood when I explained why. She didn't fall for Mike's pleading that it wasn't fair because "none of the rocks hit Dennis."

That afternoon was the first time Mike and I ended our outing without scheduling the next one. What we did schedule was "a meeting" in four days for Mike, Betty, and me to talk things over. It turned out well. Mike apologized and promised he would behave when we were on outings. He seemed relieved when the meeting ended by scheduling another outing.

****

"This is you," I said as I drew, pointing at the smaller of the two stick figures. "And right here . . . ?"

"That's you!" Mike laughed.

The stick figure guys were indistinguishable, but their positions in the roughly drawn canoe made it obvious who was who.

"And what is this, Mike?"

He stared at the bizarre figure rising out of the waves behind the canoe.

"That's . . . That's the Monster!" he chimed in.

"Right. The Loch Ness Monster."

Betty usually observed our interaction. Each time we created our calendar masterpiece, she sat quietly watching and smiling.

"We were talking about the Loch Ness Monster," I explained to Betty. "Fortunately, we escaped."

"Yeah. Him chase us all over!" Mike exclaimed.

"It was fun, wasn't it, Mike."

"Yeah. But we wasn't scared."

When our day spent paddling canoes near the University of Washington was successfully recorded on our calendar, it was time for me to head home. It had gone well. Mike continued to honor his promise to behave in the months following our "meeting," and things felt on track in our relationship as "Brothers."

"How about next Tuesday, does that work, Mike? Can I pick you up at school?"

I handed the calendar back to Mike, who studied the new stick figure drawing then flipped back through pages of previous drawings. When he finally set the calendar aside, Mike and Jake the Poodle walked me to the door. After a hug, our special handshake, and one last pet for Jake, we called it a day. I felt that Mike and I were making progress.

8

Riding the Waves

When a Little Brother's nickname is "The Fish" a boat was the best toy his Big Brother could own. Joe and I lived five miles from Lake Washington and owned a nineteen-foot Bayliner runabout. Christened *The Mud Princess* after our white Samoyed-mix dog who loved wallowing in mud, the boat was perfect for exploring Seattle's Lake Washington and Lake Union.

Boating was a great way to spend a summer afternoon, and *The Mud Princess* ended up having an unorthodox crew. A week after I met Mike, Joe was also matched with a Little Brother named Nate. A month older than Mike, Nate was an only child living with his mom in north Seattle. Nate was a high-energy, intelligent, fun-loving kid with a great sense of humor. When applying to become a Little Brother, Nate was asked what kind of Big Brother he would like. Nate responded that he wanted "a ten-year-old." Thus, the match with Joe. It turned out to be a fantastic pairing.

Joe and I often coordinated our Big Brother outings to take Nate and Mike out on the boat together. We would pack a lunch, launch the boat at Magnuson Park, and motor off without a planned destination. Eventually we cut the engine and spent a few hours floating around.

The four of us spent hours leaping in and out of the water, swimming and just hanging out. Nate always brought along a football, tossing a pass over the water for anyone jumping in to try to catch.

Mike's favorite routine was to hop into the water and stay there. Hence "The Fish" nickname. Regardless of the lake temperature, he loved swimming. At the end of the afternoon, we had to beg him to get out.

Both Little Brothers loved driving the boat. On every trip, we let them roar around on the lake like maniacs.

"Let them have some fun," Joe would say.

"They are going to kill us," I answered.

"It's good for them. They won't hit anything way out here!"

Joe was a firm believer that the Little Brothers should enjoy the parent-free time these outings gave them. So there they were, taking turns at the helm of a boat roaring full throttle over the waves, supervised by two Big Brothers who both grew up driving their family boats that way.

During breaks from swimming, both kids tried tubing. This consisted of being dragged behind the boat as a Big Brother zipped them from one side of the wake to the other. Mike would grin from ear to ear, fearless, as he was whipped around and occasionally thrown out of the tube by a rogue wave. Nate was much more cautious. He favored riding the tube at a crawl, moving along so slowly that rowing shells often passed us by.

The waterfront mansions lining the shoreline were showpieces, fascinating reminders of the wealthy people who resided along Lake Washington. One recurring destination at the end of each voyage was a stop on the east shore to survey the on-going construction of Bill Gates's new home. Under construction for nearly seven years, the $63 million project was immense. Nate and Mike knew who Bill Gates was, so they were intrigued watching the progress of the compound. We would cut the motor, float offshore, and scope out what headway had been made since our last visit.

"Can you believe that place?" Nate exclaimed.

"Check it out," Joe replied. "They are building right back into the hillside."

"Does him live there?" Mike inquired.

"Not yet," I said. "When it is finished, he will."

Nate stared at the work-site.

"Man, he has so much money! Joe, what would you do with all that money?"

"Spend it. Every dime of it!"

"Wow. I can't believe he has so much money," Nate marveled.

"I think it is going to have a garage to hold twenty cars, and a gym too," Joe said.

"Who needs all that money?" All Nate could see onshore were dollar signs.

Once the boat drifted closer to shore, we knew it was time to wrap up our day.

"Hey, guys, it's time to head home," I said.

"You know what that means!" Joe hollered.

On cue, each of us sprang up and did a cannon ball into the water. We stayed in for a few minutes, dog-paddling around and laughing. Then we climbed aboard *The Mud Princess*, fired up the engine, and darted back toward home.

An hour later, Mike's hair was still damp from our afternoon at the lake as we sat on Betty's couch. Jake the Poodle, the brown Standard Poodle Mike received for his birthday, sat in front of me smacking me non-stop with his paw, requesting pats. On the calendar, I drew four stick figure heads bobbing above some squiggly lines that represented waves. Behind them an oversized house with no roof towered on the shore. Mike laughed at the picture, then grabbed the calendar and walked over to Betty and showed it to her.

"What is it?" she asked.

"That is us and Nate and Joe, in the lake," Mike chuckled.

"And what are you doing? Swimming?"

"No. We was in the lake," he explained. "And we was all peeing in Bill Gates's pool!"

Betty stared at me. I shrugged my shoulders and smiled.

"It's a tradition."

She rolled her eyes, but her smile gave her away. I felt like all three of us were getting closer with every visit, and my time with Mike was having a positive influence. Mike was comfortable sharing time with Joe and Nate, and I noticed Nate going out of his way to help Mike and treat him well. It felt satisfying all the way around.

9

'Twas The Week Before Christmas

Mike was nestled next to my sister Peggy in the kitchen breakfast nook. She was in town to celebrate our mutual December birthdays. We were having an early dinner with Mike before he and I went to the Big Brothers office. We were scheduled to have our official match review meeting with a Big Brothers caseworker to assess our first year together.

"Peggy?"

"Yes, Mike?" She was so gentle with him.

"Peggy, do-do you think Santa Claus is real?"

She looked at me for help. I ignored her and waited to see how she wiggled her way out of this.

"Uh, yes, Mike. Yes, Santa is real," she answered hesitantly.

"Really? You think Santa Claus, you think him is real?"

"Yes." Once again Peggy looked at me for some help. *Sorry, sis, I'm having too much fun listening.*

Do you think Santa Claus is real? Mike had thrown the same question at me three weeks ago. He was on a quest to find the true answer that would have life-altering consequences for a vulnerable eight-year-old.

"I don't know, Mike. What do you think?"

"I know that him is not real."

"Why do you say that?"

"Because one time I saw Linda had some stuff. And Linda said it was from Santa. But I know it was from her. So I know that Santa, that him is not real."

It was a mighty confession. The kid was putting his yearly haul of presents from Santa on the table and rolling the dice. Here he was, risking the winner's haul by saying he didn't believe in the game.

I had a flashback of Mrs. Daugherty, my first-grade teacher, standing in front of our class. "You all know there is no such thing as Santa!" she blurted out.

For a six-year-old, it was crushing news. I rushed home from school and demanded an explanation. So when Mike asked what I thought about Santa, I passed along the advice my parents gave me.

"Well, Mike, that's okay. But I don't want you telling any other kids there's no Santa. Because if they still believe in him and you tell them, it will ruin their Christmas. Do you understand?"

"Yeah. But I know that Santa Claus, that him is not real."

"Well, some kids don't, so don't say anything."

Since that conversation, Mike had brought up the Santa topic a couple more times. He was fishing for clarity, and decided to get an outside opinion from Peggy. Obviously, as Christmas got closer, he was getting cold feet and worried about getting cut out of Santa's gift pipeline this Christmas.

"Well, Peggy. I know Santa, that him is not real." His response to her lacked the conviction it did a few weeks ago. It was time to help my sister out.

"I think Mike is asking you because he knows about Santa. But I told him telling other kids might ruin their Christmas."

"Oh yes." Peggy exhaled, and her shoulders dropped back to a normal level. "Actually, Mike, I know about Santa too, but thanks for not saying anything in case I didn't."

****

Betty and I had been chatting for nearly an hour since Mike went into the office with our Big Brothers caseworker. The match review was set up for each of us to meet individually with the caseworker. Betty had already had her meeting and finished in fifteen minutes. I would go when Mike returned.

"Are you and Joe coming over on Christmas?" Betty asked. "We'd love to have you."

"We're planning on it. I think that—"

"Excuse me."

It was the caseworker. Mike was standing in the doorway next to her, sobbing.

"We are going to end our review for tonight," the caseworker said firmly.

"What's wrong?" Betty asked as she walked over to comfort Mike.

"It's okay, honey. Come on. Let's walk down here," Betty said, taking his hand, and Mike grabbed her tightly as they stepped into the hall.

"What happened?" I asked the caseworker.

"Well . . ." The caseworker was hesitant, choosing her words carefully. "We have some questions we go over with the Little Brothers. One question is if he and his Big Brother have any secrets. Mike said that you two have a secret, and he won't tell me what it is."

"What?" I was floored. *Where the hell did that come from?* "We don't have any secrets."

"He says you do. But he wouldn't tell me what the secret is. He just keeps crying."

It was clear she suspected me of child abuse.

"Did he say anything else?"

"Not really. We were talking about things, a little about Christmas, and he asked me about Santa. He said you two had a secret. Then he started crying."

"Wait a minute," I said, holding up my hand. "Did he ask if you believed in Santa?"

"Yes. He asked if I thought Santa Claus was real."

"And what did you say?"

"I said yes, that I thought Santa was real."

"That's the secret. Mike knows Santa isn't real, and I told him not to tell other kids because it might ruin their Christmas. You told him Santa was real, so he thinks you believe in him. And he's not going to tell you his secret, because it will ruin your Christmas."

"Santa?" She looked baffled. This was not what she suspected.

"Ask him. I bet any amount of money that's his secret."

When Betty and Mike returned, the caseworker asked Mike if she could talk to him. He looked to Betty for reassurance.

"It's okay, Mike. I'll be right here."

"I can't figure it out," Betty said when they left the room. "He kept crying and mumbling about Santa."

"She asked him if we had any secrets," I told Betty. "They suspect me of sexual abuse because Mike told her that we had a secret but wouldn't budge when she wanted to know what it was."

"Secrets?"

"Yes, it's really an innocent one. The secret is just Santa Claus. Mike asked her if she thought Santa was real, and she said yes. Mike thinks she believes in him and he's not about to tell her Santa is fake. I told him not to tell other kids because he could ruin their Christmas."

As frivolous as Mike's secret seemed, this was a loaded situation. Mike's speech difficulties made conversation with him extremely challenging. Rather than ask for Betty's help to try to sort out what Mike was talking about, the caseworker was convinced it was a serious problem and shut down the review session. Her quick leap from secret to possible abuse was not surprising, but given the agency's recent record of blocking gay volunteers in order to prevent sexual abuse, it was alarming.

Mike told the caseworker his secret once she told him she didn't believe in Santa. She seemed relieved, but she still ended our meeting. I walked away that evening very unsettled. I saw there were clear risks presented by having a suspicious caseworker interrogate a Little Brother with serious speech issues. That risk added an edge of caution to every conversation I had with any of the caseworkers from that point forward.

10

A Morning Chat

I have wonderful memories of visiting Betty and having coffee in her kitchen nook overlooking the courtyard. Those were relaxed mornings when I had the day off, Mike was at school, and Betty and I had plenty of time to shoot the breeze. It was a great way to get to know her better.

"So you were Mike's foster mom starting when he was two years old?"

"Yes. I did daycare, and I'd get foster kids in occasionally. They usually came needing an emergency placement, and that's how Mike showed up. I got a call asking if I had space to keep a toddler for a couple days."

"Did he just stay here from then on?"

"No. He was here a few days, then was returned to his biological mother. Several weeks later they brought him back here again, and after a short stay they again sent him back to his mother. Then it started to happen frequently, always bringing him here, then eventually giving him back to her."

"What was the problem with his mother?"

"She was unstable. She had four other kids, all girls who had already been removed from her before she had Mike. Every time there was a crisis, Mike came back to me. Once he showed up with a broken arm. Another time there was a pack of paperwork mixed in with his clothes. Inside the envelope was a photograph of Mike lying naked on a bed with candles burning all around him. Who knows what was really going on with her? Whatever she was up to, it wasn't good."

A MORNING CHAT

"Damn! Why did they kept giving him back to her?"

"Because she still had parental rights. She would clean up her act, convince the court she could care for him, and they'd give Mike back to her. One time the court gave him back to his mother, then a couple hours later she called the police, said she didn't want him anymore, and told the cops to come get him."

I was horrified to hear what Mike had gone through.

"By then Mike was getting bounced around so much I was afraid he would get lost in the foster system. So I looked into getting guardianship, which finally happened."

"What happened to his mother?"

"She ended up in prison. She'd started harassing me and a psychologist who had worked with her. I got weird phone calls all the time, then it turned into threats. Mike's mother knew where I lived but luckily never showed up there. The psychologist was getting the same calls and wasn't about to put up with it. She pressed charges, and Mike's mother was sent to prison. Which is where she belongs."

"Is she there now?"

"I'm not sure. I haven't heard from her, don't know where she is, and I don't want to."

"Does Mike remember her?"

"Yes. Occasionally he mentions her name, but I doubt he'd recognize her."

"Wow, he had it rough. What a blessing he landed here with you."

"It was horrible to see him in that situation. He's such a good kid."

I could feel the tension in Betty's voice as she talked about the mother's threats. Now I understood her motivation for the recent move into this home located a couple miles away from where she lived when I first met Mike. This house had two living areas. Betty and Mike occupied the main and upper floors, Linda and her family resided on the lower level.

Betty loved the new place. It had a nice view, plenty of room, and she enjoyed the companionship of Linda and her family. Best of all, it gave her peace of mind that Mike's biological mother no longer knew where she and Mike lived.

11

Not Shicken—Chicken!

"Was that at school?" I asked.

"No. It wa-wa... It wa-was by the..."

The afternoon had turned into a tough juggling act. I was trying to drive and decipher Mike's speech as the gears between his mind and mouth were grinding to a painful halt.

"By Ma—Mac..." he tried again. "By Mac, MacDon—"

Suddenly he was quiet. The sound of his mangled speech was replaced by sobs of frustration that no matter how hard he tried, the words just would not come out.

My eyes shifted off the traffic for a second. Mike had turned away and with every sob was shrinking a bit further into a fetal position. Other cars kept buzzing around us, passing drivers giving me a look that said: *Get the hell out of the way!*

The parking lot of a small store finally offered us refuge from the overwhelming pressure. Mike then erupted into a total meltdown.

I put my hand on his shoulder and let him cry. On these days, the pain he felt about his speech struggles also pushed a button inside me.

"Are you having a hard time with your speech today, buddy?"

Rapid, deep sobs were the only response.

"It feels pretty hard, doesn't it?"

"Uh-huh."

I rubbed his shoulder and let him continue crying.

"Mike?" I finally said. "Can you look at me for a minute?"

He turned slowly. The corners of his mouth were pulled down in a painful grimace. Pain covered his red, wet face. He slowly wiped tears from his face with the inside of his arm.

"Buddy, I know it's hard. I really wish I could fix it for you."

He sniffled, trying hard to stifle another sob.

"If I could fix it for you, I would."

The floodgate of tears opened wide again.

"I am proud of you, Mike, because I know you work very, very hard on your speech. All you can do is keep working, buddy." I rubbed his shoulder a bit more. "You keep trying and working hard, and I promise you it will get better."

Or would it? The odds were stacked against him ever developing normal speech. It was going to be a life-long challenge. I didn't want to lie to him, but what good would it do to tell him the truth?

Whenever Mike spoke to people, their stunned expression was so discouraging. Instinctively their gaze shifted from Mike to me. After just a couple words from Mike, it was easy to read their thoughts: *What's wrong with him?* If I could sense that, I knew Mike could too.

The determined courage Mike showed in trying to communicate inspired me. The best I could do was to help him learn to manage it. When we went out, I made him tell the clerks or servers what he wanted. It was painful to watch, and often called for some translation, yet bit by bit he was gaining some confidence speaking. Then a day like this would hit and his speech difficulty slugged Mike with a vengeance.

"Mike, did I ever tell you that I had to go to speech therapy too?"

"You did?"

"Yep. Didn't I ever tell you that?"

"No. Really?"

"Yeah. And you know what? I HATED it!"

"You did?"

"Yep. I was in second grade. I couldn't make 'S' sounds right. So I had to go to speech therapy after school. I was so embarrassed I didn't tell anyone. Not even my brothers and sisters."

"Really?"

"Yeah. Every time I said an 'S', the sound would come out the side of my mouth."

"You did?"

"I sure did. They made me read all these stupid stories, stuff where every word had an 'S' in it."

I began slurring my sounds, exaggerating them so they came out the side of my mouth.

"'Sally Sharp said she should send some socks to Sam Smith. So Sally Sharp sent some speckled socks so Sam Smith's shoes shouldn't stay so stinky and smelly.'"

Mike smiled and chuckled.

"And my teacher would yell, 'NO! Make the sound come out the FRONT!'"

I put my face close to Mike and started hissing S's without stopping. "S,S,S,S . . . Sam Smith said smelly shoes seem so sweet; so Sam Smith suggests Sally Sharp stop sending speckled socks. Sam says Sally Sharp should simply shove it!"

Mike snickered. "Really? You had speech?"

"Yep. I felt like a snake! I hated S's, Mike, and I still do," I hissed. "And you know what, Mike?"

"What?"

"Sometimes when I'm talking, I still have to remind myself to say the sound right. And I haven't been to speech for a long, long time!"

"Oh. You do?" My confession about my own speech problems was lifting his spirits. It was something we really had in common.

"Yep. I couldn't say the 'CH' sound either, like in 'chicken.' It would come out *shicken*. 'I want shicken! Give me some shicken!' And you know what happened?"

"What?"

"I had to say 'chicken' so many times when I was a kid that now when I go to a restaurant, what do I order? Chicken!"

His eyes sparkled. Something had clicked during this conversation; his frustration had evaporated.

"So you just keep working, Mike. Practice and work hard with your speech teacher. I was embarrassed about my speech when I was a kid too. But if you keep working it can get better."

"Okay," he exhaled. "Promise?"

"Yes. I know it's hard, like when we order at McDonald's. But you keep trying, okay?"

"Yeah." He relaxed. There was an ease in his body language that had been missing for a while.

"And one more thing, buddy?"

"What?"

"Always order the shicken," I said, "Say 'I want the shicken! Gimme the DAMN SHICKEN!'"

Laughter filled the truck, and it felt wonderful. The kid had a ton of courage, and I admired him. Watching him wrestle through life reminded me how insignificant any of my struggles were.

I gave Mike a big hug and got rewarded with a heartwarming smile. I had to admit that making him feel better made me feel great. I turned the radio up loud and revved up the engine, then Mike and I screeched onto the street and back into the fast lane.

12

The Speedometer

There are a few gifts for a kid that, in the moment, seem like a brilliant idea. One of those was a bike speedometer. This can't-miss gift was simple. It was inexpensive, and even a technically challenged guy like me could hook it up without too much trouble. A little digital speedometer would be a simple way for a kid like Mike, whose fascination with distance and speed had taken up hours of our conversations, to keep track of "how far, how fast".

Many of our afternoons were spent biking together along Seattle's Burke-Gilman trail. For Mike, the speedometer seemed to be the perfect addition to the twenty-inch bike Betty bought him. For me, it could best be described as a brain fart.

Nowhere in the speedometer installation instructions (or the accompanying product warnings) was there any mention of riding ability. Mike loved to just chug along and take in the scenery as he rode. He could either be totally focused or easily distracted, neither one an asset while riding on busy bike paths.

Behind the handlebars of a bike, Mike was a crash waiting to happen. When something on the side of the trail would catch his attention, his eyes would lock on it, pulling his head and then his entire upper body to the side. This led him to either careen off the trail, or worse yet, plow into oncoming riders.

We had many close calls. The thought that there might be danger ahead was something Mike could never grasp. Until he smashed head-on into something, it was impossible for him to notice it was even approaching.

Those were details I forgot the day I plunked down my money for his bike speedometer. I thought he would love watching the number of miles he pedaled add up, but I neglected to calculate road hazards like distraction and gravity.

****

One afternoon, Mike and I joined Nate and Joe for a bike ride through the Seattle Arboretum. Mike struggled trying to match Nate's athletic abilities. The two kids were on opposite ends of the spectrum when it came to physical strength and coordination. With every twist and turn along the paths, Mike's frustration grew. I was working overtime trying to be encouraging.

"Careful, Mike! Slow down, buddy!"

But he tuned out my warning, focused on catching up to Joe and Nate as they zipped along.

When the four of us stopped at the top of a hill, we could see my truck parked in a gravel lot next to the paved road that led to the bottom of the hill. All that stood between us and the end of a successful outing was one steep descent.

Nate zipped down first, easily navigating the sharp turn near the bottom. His cautious nature tempered his athletic ability enough to keep his speed in check. He made the ride down easily. Joe flew down behind Nate and joined him at the bottom.

Right beside me, with his solid frame plopped on his little bike, was Mike. His helmet was on tight, his eyes locked on the road.

"Be careful, Mike, this road is very steep," I warned. "You've got to go slow."

"Okay," he mumbled.

Mike launched himself down the hill, and I followed close behind.

"Mike," I yelled. "Slow down. Mike! SLOW DOWN!"

Maybe he didn't hear me, maybe it didn't matter. The curve didn't matter. People standing in the gravel lot at the bottom of the hill didn't matter.

All that mattered was his shiny new speedometer! Like a carnival character shot from a cannon, Mike flew down the hill at breakneck speed, head down, eyes glued to the flashing numbers on the gadget I had mounted on his handlebars.

Suddenly, Mike couldn't pedal fast enough to keep up with the gravity! But those jumping numbers on the speedometer fascinated him as he entered the curve. He veered left, overcorrected toward the right, then turned sharply back to the left. His bike wobbled and his feet left the pedals. The front wheel abruptly turned sideways, the back of the bike pitched forward and Mike catapulted over the top of the handlebars. He skidded across the pavement, grinding to a stop face down in the gravel.

"MIKE!" I screamed. "Are you okay?"

Blood streamed from out of his arms, legs, and face. He struggled to stand up. I was so relieved to see he could move. *Oh my God!* I thought. He could have been paralyzed, and it would have been my fault.

"Are you okay?"

He nodded, blood running from his nose.

Joe grabbed a first aid kit from the truck, and both of us worked on Mike. We wiped away the blood, and, thank God, below the mess it didn't look like he was seriously injured. Nothing was broken.

"Where does it hurt, Mike?" Joe asked.

Mike looked right at us, beaming.

"I was going sixty miles an hour!"

"Yeah, you were going fast, Mike. You crashed hard," Joe said.

"I was going sixty!" he bragged. "I was! I looked and it said sixty!"

"Does this hurt?" I asked, checking his arm, his legs, feeling so guilty.

"Did you know I could go up to sixty? How fast was you going?" Speed was all he cared about, the sight of the flashing "60" on his new speedometer just before he crashed.

"Sixty miles an hour? There's no way!" Nate growled. "No way, Mike!"

"I was too going sixty! It said sixty on my speedometer!" Mike insisted.

"You were going real fast, Mike," I agreed, trying to distract him. "Here, let's put a bandage on that leg."

Nate was not going to let it pass.

"MICHAEL, IF YOU WERE GOING SIXTY MILES AN HOUR, YOU'D

THE SPEEDOMETER

BE DEAD!" Nate hollered.

"Hey, Nate, give me a hand with these," Joe said, changing the subject. He took Nate to the truck and loaded up the bikes before a war broke out.

Fortunately, we had driven two vehicles to the Arboretum. With Nate still fuming about Mike's sixty miles an hour, he and Joe got into the Ford Explorer and drove away.

I helped Mike hobble to my truck and settle in for the ride home. I was so glad he was in one piece; I felt responsible for getting him the damn speedometer, and now it was broken in the wreck. How was I going to explain this to Betty?

I looked over at Mike. Despite the scratches and cuts, his face was plastered with a big smile.

"Did you see me? I was going sixty miles an hour!" In Mike's mind, we had just wrapped up a perfect day.

13

Liar! Liar!

The glory of spending an afternoon with my Little Brother was that I never had a clue what was going to happen. On this particular day I took a break from rushing around preparing to leave town on a work trip. I picked Mike up from school, and fate took it from there. There was no way to plan for what would come up in the afternoon's conversation.

"You lie-lied!" His voice was emphatic, even through his stuttering. "You, you said that w-we was going to go do it on Wednesday. Is today Wednesday?"

"No, Mike. Today is Tuesday."

"See? You lied! You said Wednesday, and you was lying. And my teacher lied, and Betty lied to me, too."

Everybody was lying. That was a problem, because every conversation with Mike during the past two weeks led to him accusing someone of lying. He asked a question and found a minor inconsistency or change of plans. Immediately he got angry about the "lie" and started carrying on.

"Mike, you seem upset. What's wrong?"

"You lied! You said Wednesday, but it's Tuesday." He folded his arms over his chest and stared out the passenger-side window.

"Mike, I told you when I called you Sunday that my work schedule changed. I'll be gone tomorrow. That was why we changed our day to today."

"You lied! You said Wednesday!"

He was angry, and he was really pissing me off. It was all I could do to keep

LIAR! LIAR!

my cool while I was wracking my brain to figure out what was sending him into a tizzy.

"Mike, do you want to talk? If something is wrong, maybe I can help."

"No. Let's talk about some—something else." He pointed out the window. "See that, the dog. We, I want . . . talk about the dog!"

"Okay, buddy. I won't ask again. Let's go get a snack, and then we'll go to the park. If you want to talk, just let me know."

"Yeah."

****

We were still in the parking lot of 7-Eleven, Mike holding an unopened box of Junior Mints. I was just breaking into my Reese's Peanut Butter Cups when he spoke up.

"Okay. I will tell you."

That was quick! His decision to talk put me on the defensive. I needed to be careful, to respond appropriately.

"All right," I inquired. "What is it?"

"I had sex with Christina on the school bus."

"What?"

"I had sex with Christina on the school bus," he repeated confidently.

I almost choked on my candy. The "I had sex" didn't surprise me. It was the "on the school bus" that threw me for a loop.

Mike was bused to school on one of the distinctive small school buses used for special needs students; a so-called short bus. Six rows of windows, four rows of seats, and extra space in the rear to accommodate students using wheelchairs. Or for students to use while having sex, apparently.

Mike stared at me. He wanted a response.

But I was occupied with a mental porn show running through my mind. Images of every sexual position I had ever heard of, imagined, or even tried filled my head. For the life of me, I couldn't pick out a single one that would work for two students riding a short bus. Unless the driver was blind, there was no way they would miss the fact that Mike and Christina were studying anatomy together.

"How did you have sex on the school bus?"

His eyes narrowed and he stared right at me. "You know how to do it, don't you?"

"Y-yes," I stammered. "Yes, I know how to do it."

I hoped he didn't notice I was blushing. Another question like that and I would definitely choke on my candy. I was doomed if Mike got focused on this line of questioning. There was no way I was going to spend this January afternoon explaining my sex life to my Little Brother.

"I mean, uh . . ." I stammered. "Mike, what exactly do you mean when you say that you had sex on the school bus?"

"Me and Christina, we was on the bus. And—and then her put her hands into my pants."

"While you were on the bus?" The picture was getting clearer. So was Mike's conscience. The tension in his face melted as he talked.

"Yeah."

"Oh, I see. When did this happen, Mike?" I was trying to be gentle with him, knowing this was huge in his mind.

"Before my vacation."

Before his vacation. He had been wrestling with this nasty little secret since before Christmas break.

"Well, I'm glad you told me, Mike."

"I'm glad I tell you too."

"Did you tell Betty?"

Dead silence. He was thinking.

"Her ask me what happened," he said softly. "I say nothing happen."

"So she doesn't know about it?"

"No."

"Well, I think it's important to let Betty know, so she can help you if you have questions." *Fat chance. What kid is going to run his sex life by his mom?*

"I'm glad you told me, Mike. When things like that happen, it's a good idea to talk with Betty or me instead of keeping it secret. We can help you with it."

"Okay," he sighed.

"And Mike, it's probably a good idea to wait until you are older to experiment with sex."

"I, I know I shouldn't do it. But Christina . . .her, her kept asking for me to do it."

"It's okay to tell Christina no." His body language changed as if the weight of the world had been lifted off his shoulders.

"Thanks for telling me, Mike." I reached over and put my hand on his shoulder. "Now, how about if we go to the park and hang out."

"Okay." A smile of relief covered his face.

This is exactly why I am a Big Brother.

****

It was dark when we headed back toward Betty's. Mike and I spent the afternoon in Seattle's Magnuson Park, walking along logs lining the park roads. We pretended that a slip off a log would throw us into imaginary hot lava that flowed everywhere below us. It was a dangerous threat. Yet as in any storybook adventure, tragedy was short-lived. If we fell into the lava, we just hopped up and started over.

"Hey, Mike?" We hadn't mentioned the sex on the school bus since we left 7-Eleven.

"Huh?"

"Mike, I think you need to tell Betty what happened with Christina. When we get home, you have a choice. We can talk to her together, or you can tell her after I leave. If you do that, I will call her when I get home to be sure you told her."

"We tell her together." He knew his odds for survival when mom got bad news improved greatly if Big Brother was with him.

Jake the Poodle spun, barked, and peed all over the floor to welcome us home. Betty was settled in her easy chair enjoying the twinkling view of the Seattle skyline. She slid an ashtray full of cigarette butts over and set her crossword book on the end table.

Mike grabbed his calendar, and we plopped down on the couch. Jake immediately smacked me with his paw, wanting to be petted. Mike sat beside me and watched the stick figures emerge on the calendar page. The tall figure walked along the log, not noticing the short one behind was flailing on one leg about to plunge into lava. As I drew, we told Betty about our adventures at the park.

Then it was time.

"Betty, something came up today that Mike wants to tell you about." I glanced at him.

He didn't look concerned when I mentioned it. "Go ahead, Mike."

"Uh. Me, me. I had. . . Christina and me. We had sex."

"WHAT?" Betty gasped.

"Me and Christina, we had sex . . . on the bus." Mike looked away from Betty and up at me. "You tell her!"

"Mike told me that a couple weeks ago Christina put her hand in his pants on the school bus."

"Yeah," Mike added, nodding.

"Mike," Betty's voice intensified, "didn't we talk about Christina?" Her reaction was stronger than in any of our earlier "what-the-kid-did-now" conversations.

"Uh-huh," Mike mumbled.

"And what did I say about Christina?"

"You say. You told me to stay away. Stay away from Christina."

"That's right. And did you do that?"

"No."

"You need to stay away from Christina. Do you understand?" Just the name Christina seemed to get Betty fired up.

"Okay." He hung his head.

"And if Christina bothers you, you need to tell her to stop."

"Uh . . . Okay."

"I told Mike he had to tell you about this," I added. "I let him know he should ask you if he has any questions. I wanted to make sure you knew."

Betty and I shared a smile. I knew she was relieved to find out what had been bothering him recently.

"We have talked about Christina before," Betty sighed, shaking her head. Right then I knew that the next time the short bus arrived to pick up Mike, Christina was going to get an earful from Betty.

"Mike, why did you tell Dennis about this but you didn't tell me?"

"I tell him because him is my trusted friend," Mike responded.

Him is my trusted friend. A wave of gratitude flowed over me when Mike said that. His trust reassured me that our time together was helping him, and I was doing a good job being a friend.

14

My Special Christmas Gift

From my spot on the slate ledge of the fireplace, I had an unobstructed view of the holiday celebration winding down. Dinner was over and the final bits of clean-up were underway. The sugar rush from dessert was momentarily saving me from the food coma I knew would hit. This was a glorious time of any holiday, that peaceful transition as a hectic day slowly shifted into a carefree, mellow flow.

The warm fire massaged my back as I watched Betty's family members share conversations. Eleven of us had gathered at her home to celebrate Christmas Eve, and Joe, Mike, me, and Jake the Poodle were the only ones that were not smoking. A thick fog of cigarette smoke choked the living and dining rooms, yet it was obvious that contentment filled the house.

The night was one of many special times Joe and I had shared with Betty and her family during the three years I had been Mike's Big Brother. Watching their interaction renewed my appreciation for the bond they shared. I knew bits and pieces of some of their family struggles, but tonight it was apparent how much they loved each other.

Betty and her daughter Linda moved continually between the dining room and the kitchen, on each trip rounding up a few plates and utensils. Betty's son Tom and his partner were washing dishes, and the conversation drifting from the kitchen was punctuated with occasional laughter.

As I watched I reflected on the support Betty had given me in my work with Mike. She was flexible, gave us freedom to do what we wanted, and appreciated my help. She not only kept Mike well behaved, Betty let Big Brother know when things were off course and I needed to right the ship.

One day I mentioned that I was wrestling with depression, that it was dragging me down. Her reply was pure no-nonsense Betty.

"Well, you just better put a firecracker up your butt and get on with life," she replied, puffing on her cigarette.

****

"Is it my turn?" Joe asked Mike.

"Yeah. You go," Mike answered. They were on the floor in front of me playing cards. With a stack of just-opened Christmas gifts stacked beside him as he hung out with Joe, Mike was in his glory. He was lying on his stomach, balancing on his elbows. The carefree kicking motion of his legs announced to everyone that he was very, very happy. As I watched them play cards, I thought of all the progress Mike and I had made during the past few years. He had learned to read, mastered various video games, and could play a killer game of chess.

He had slowly made strides in his speech, working hard to improve his word formation and vocabulary to communicate a thought whenever he got stuck. His frustrated crying spells around his speech stopped, and he was able to cope much better. Despite his progress, Mike's communication challenges could never be entirely fixed.

Wham! A neatly trimmed brown paw with long black nails landed another hit on my leg. Jake was always pestering me for attention. Each time I visited, the beautiful brown Standard Poodle was on a nonstop crusade to get petted. He could be a pest, but I considered him a kindred spirit. Since the day he arrived at Betty's as a puppy on Mike's eighth birthday, Jake and I both shared Mike's friendship. He supported Betty in her day-to-day work raising Mike, and I had a lot of respect for Betty and Jake.

"One more game?" Mike asked, hoping his games with Joe would never end.

"Okay, this is the last one," Joe replied with a smile. This was where the real competition started, when negotiations about ending the games got serious.

It would be Mike's dogged persistence pitted against Joe's unlimited patience. Mike had the edge because his natural sweetness tugged on Joe's heartstrings, making it nearly impossible for him to tell Mike no. Joe usually let Mike win, and the shot of self-confidence was adding to the magic of Mike's night.

The final game ended quickly.

"I'm the champ!" Mike exclaimed.

"Good job!" Joe said, and shook his hand.

As soon as Joe disappeared into the veil of smoke coming from the kitchen, the pile of gifts grabbed Mike's attention. I watched him examine the presents until Jake demanded to be petted.

"Okay, you pest. Doesn't anyone ever pet you?"

Mike set one of his new books on top of his gift pile and moved toward the fireplace. He sat down next to me and snuggled up closely.

"Thank you for the video game."

"You're welcome, Mike."

"It was what I really wanted."

"You are a great kid, and you deserve it."

Mike edged closer, then looked directly into my eyes.

"I love you. I love you more than all the Christmas presents I ever got."

I was surprised. His words were simple, sincere, and powerful, and they touched my heart deeply.

"I love you too, Mike. I'm so glad you are my Little Brother."

15

The Sneak Attack

Big Brothers had moved to a new office in Seattle's Central District since I was matched with Mike. The new digs were modern, with abundant windows that added a refreshing, open feel. It was a welcome change from the dreary, old school building that housed the agency during the days of "we are looking for heterosexual role models for our kids."

My caseworker had called and asked me to come in so we could have a little review of our match. She was the same woman who had conducted the Santa Claus interview during our first match review. Since that debacle, the review sessions were held over the phone.

After exchanging pleasantries, she got right to the point.

"I have a question I need to ask."

"Sure, what's up?"

"Did you and Michael do an overnight stay with your sister a while back?"

"Yes. Mike, Nate, Joe, and I went to Fort Lewis in Tacoma. My nephew, who both Mike and Nate have met before, had a Little League baseball game. We had arranged with Betty and Nate's mother Jean that we would go down for the game, stay with my sister, let the kids watch movies and hang out, then head home the next morning."

"Did you get approval from our office for the overnight?"

"No. We cleared it with both their mothers. They both have met my sister and her son. They were good with it. I wasn't aware we needed to check with the office. Why?"

"Well, we have decided that we are going to terminate your Big Brother match. We think you are getting too involved in the kids' lives."

"What did you say?"

"We think you are getting too involved in the kids' lives."

"Who? Who thinks I am getting too involved in the kids' lives? You?"

"We talked it over. We are going to terminate your match."

"We who? You and Betty talked it over?"

"No, the staff here."

"And what did Betty say when you talked to her?"

"We haven't talked with Betty. We'll do that after this meeting."

"Wait a minute. You're telling me you are ending the match. You never contacted me to ask about your concerns. You haven't talked to Betty. You just made an assumption that I'm 'too involved' so you called me in to terminate the match?"

"Yes. And Joe is going to get the same call this afternoon."

"And what about Mike and Nate?"

"They will be given the option to be rematched."

"Meaning you'll put them on the list of kids waiting for other volunteers. With hundreds of other boys who are still waiting because there aren't enough volunteers, correct?"

"Uh, yes."

"I can't believe this. We cleared this with their moms, just like every outing either of us has done with them over the past three years. You didn't even bother to talk with their mothers about the situation or ask Joe or me about it. You just terminate two very successful matches."

"Yes."

It was hogwash. "We think you are getting too involved" actually meant "We think you are a risk for committing sexual abuse."

It's a given that any agency dealing with kids needs to be hyper vigilant about potential abuse. Especially an agency like Big Brothers of King County, which had been sued over an abuse case. I understood that and supported it completely.

THE SNEAK ATTACK

What I also understood was that I was dealing with an agency that spent years recruiting only "heterosexual role models" for their kids. The King County Big Brothers chapter had been one of a handful in the entire nation that chose to discriminate against gay volunteers as a way to prevent sex abuse. Even though that official policy had changed, I was aware there was a holdover of fear about gay volunteers that still affected this agency. I experienced it firsthand in the knee jerk reaction my caseworker had to the Santa Claus "secret." She suspected abuse and slammed our match review meeting to a halt. Now I was seeing it again as the agency's decision makers (most of whom worked here during the "no gays allowed" years) chose to terminate our matches without talking to the moms or Big Brother volunteers for clarification. There was no question in my mind that this situation would have been handled differently if we were heterosexual.

****

Joe was shocked when I got home and filled him in on the meeting. As promised, Big Brothers called him that afternoon to terminate his match with Nate. I called Betty and let her know what had gone on. She had not heard anything from Big Brothers and told me she would keep me posted.

I was furious. For three years I had been consistent in doing outings with Mike every other week. Together we had done a myriad of activities, including Big Brother group activities and community service projects with other matches. I had worked closely with Betty and kept her aware of any issues that arose in our outings. Mike's personality and disabilities required a huge amount of patience, understanding, and consistency on our outings. That time was shared with him in the hope it would help him feel better about life and himself. To have the caseworker call me in and tell me they were terminating the match because I was "too involved" was an insult.

Shortly after both Joe and I were told our matches were being closed, the agency spoke to Betty and Nate's mother. I have no idea what was said, but I'm sure the Big Brothers staff got an earful from both of them. A few days later, our caseworkers called both Joe and me to say our matches would continue on as before.

It was good news and a relief. Our matches continued, and both Joe and I kept up our commitment to be solid, trustworthy friends to Mike and Nate for several more years.

But from my perspective, it was impossible to continue on as before. From that point forward, I knew I had to watch my back. My trust was shattered. The situation had been badly mishandled, and the same caseworkers who had just tried to boot Joe and me out the door continued to be assigned to our matches.

16

Showgirls!

"Showgirls? Hey let's go to see the Sho-Showgirls!"

His voice was so loud that even the driver of the half-filled city bus could hear Mike, who was sitting in the last row of seats. I tried to ignore him, thankful I had taken a seat across the aisle.

Joe was not so lucky. He was stuck right next to Mike, and Nate was on the opposite window seat next to me.

"Let's go see them. The Showgirls!"

Everyone on the bus could hear him. Mike was obsessed with the flashing neon sign outside the strip club we just passed.

"Showgirls!" He looked right at Joe. "Can we go to see them?"

I looked out the window pretending I wasn't there and hoped I didn't get dragged into the conversation. It was hard not to laugh. I knew Mike was going to corner Joe with his questions. It was clear Mike had no idea what showgirls were. And he didn't have a clue about how loud he was talking.

"Can we?" he asked again, ramping up his volume. "Can we all go to see the Showgirls?"

"No, Mike," Joe responded bluntly. "We can't go see the Showgirls."

"WHY? Why can't we go see them?"

With each question Mike got louder, pushing harder and harder for the answer he wanted. Every time Mike asked another question, more passengers turned around to stare.

"Why not?"

"Because you have to be twenty-one."

Joe was trying to keep his voice low as his answers got more abrupt. Four years with Mike had thrown me into plenty of situations where I was squirming before responding to his off-the-wall suggestions. It was great to hear Mike throwing curve balls at Joe and entertaining to hear Joe get put through the wringer, I had to admit.

"Why? Why do you have to be twenty-one?" Mike demanded to know. "What do they do?"

"Uh, they dance."

Good answer, Joe.

"You watch them dance," Joe repeated softly.

"They dance?!" Mike hollered. "Do you go and watch Showgirls?"

"No."

"WHY NOT? You are over twenty-one!"

When Joe didn't answer, Mike got even louder. "Why? Why don't you? How come? Don't you want to see the Showgirls?"

I turned around and joined the rest of the passengers staring at Mike and Joe. Just who was this kid in the back row begging to go watch strippers? Mike had no clue he was providing free entertainment to every rider on the bus.

Nate's body language communicated his irritation. He hadn't said a word, but was rolling his eyes and squirming in his seat. It had taken some convincing to get Joe and Nate to agree to ride the bus with Mike and me into downtown Seattle. Mike and I saw going to the Seattle Boat Show by bus as an adventure; Nate and Joe viewed it as a waste of time.

When a guy offered us drugs while we waited for the bus home, Nate flipped into panic mode. He was happy to jump on a city bus —any bus— if it was traveling away from the streets of downtown Seattle. Then, just as Nate started to relax, we passed the Showgirls.

"Don't you like to see people dance, Joe?"

"No. I told you, Mike. I don't want to see the Showgirls."

Mike pointed over at me.

"What about HIM?" he yelled. "Does him go and see the Showgirls?"

"No, he doesn't," Joe mumbled.

"WHY?" Mike blasted the question across the aisle at me.

"Don't you like to watch people dance?"

It was a direct hit. I was stuck, and I knew I was going to have to answer. "I just don't, Mike," I said flatly.

My answer was a short explanation. The real reason: *No, Mike I'm gay! Watching Showgirls doesn't do a thing for me!*

"Well, I do!" Mike hollered. "I like to watch people dance!"

He tried me again. "Really?" he bellowed. "You don't like to see people dance?"

"No, Mike."

"WHY?" he insisted. "Don't you want to go see them, JUST FOR ONE TIME?"

"MICHAEL!" Nate glared at him and hollered, "THEY DANCE NAKED!"

"Oh!" Mike gasped.

You could have heard a rat pee on cotton. Everyone was staring at Mike. Joe looked across the aisle at Nate.

"HEY, MISTER!" Joe hollered. "HOW DO YOU KNOW THEY DANCE NAKED? DO YOU GO WATCH THE SHOWGIRLS?"

We were laughing so hard we almost missed our stop. "Take a Bus Downtown" was scratched off our collective "things to do" list.

But I knew Mike. Behind his laughter, something big was brewing in his head. He was busy scrolling through his "Must Do" list. Right below "Watch rated R-movies when I'm 17," he was adding his newest goal: "Go see the naked Showgirls!"

17

Mike's Lucky Life

"Can we watch a movie?" Mike was on a roll. He had been talking nonstop since we returned from the hotel pool.

"Ah, not tonight, Mike."

"Why? Why can't we wa-watch a movie on TV?"

"It's getting late, and we are getting up early tomorrow. Maybe tomorrow night we can."

Who could blame him for being excited? We'd flown from Seattle to Los Angeles a few hours ago. The next morning, we were heading to Disneyland. The trip was our celebration of five years as Big Brother and Little Brother, years of friendship and years of adventures.

"Did you like flying on the airplane?" I asked.

"Yeah. Did you?"

"I did; it's the best part of my job. I get to travel a lot. Do you think you might like to do that when you get older, Mike?"

"Uh, maybe."

"Do you ever think of what you would like to be when you grow up?"

"Ah. No."

For a few seconds, a weird silence hung in the room. Then Mike spoke.

"All I just want . . . I just want to be normal. I want to, to be a normal kid."

The comment hit me like a bomb.

A normal kid. He didn't want to be popular like I did when I was his age. He didn't want a new bike or a new video game. He couldn't imagine a career. He just wanted to be normal.

It was like making a birthday wish during a tornado. The kid makes a wish, and right before he blows out the candles, Mother Nature storms in and trashes the cake. The house remains standing, but the cake and the wish are nothing but smashed, scattered crumbs.

"You are a normal kid, Mike," I tried to tell him. *I'm lying. Sound convincing, Dennis.* "You are a good kid who likes things that all kids like." *I meant it, didn't I?*

"You have some challenges, Mike. But you are a normal kid."

"I have a Lucky Life," he said cheerfully. "I'm lucky! I got a good mom; I guh-got Jake, m-my dog. I got you. And my house. I got a Lucky Life."

"Me too, Mike. I have a Lucky Life too. And I'm lucky to have you as my Little Brother."

A few minutes later, Mike was sound asleep. But I kept tossing and turning. Try as I may, I couldn't forget Mike's voice.

"A Lucky Life. I got a Lucky Life."

Mike had a Lucky Life. But not a normal one.

III

Mid-Match

Uncertainty is the most stressful feeling.

18

Story of a Sinking Ship

"How about a story?" Mike asked.

"Okay. Once Upon..."

"Wait," Mike interrupted. "Have me, ha-have my dog Jake, and Medusa. And you."

"You want you, me, Jake the Poodle, and Medusa in the story?"

"Yeah. On the ship."

"The ship? Which ship?"

"The *Titanic*. That ship."

The time Mike and I had shared was wrapping up the same way most of the drives home from weekly outings did. It was time for me to tell him a story. He provided the prompts, and then plots started swirling inside my head. *Mike, his poodle, Medusa, and me. All sailing happily along together on the Titanic.*

What came to mind was a fantastic tale. An adventure that was filled with fun and driven by the exploits we shared together. In the story, we would become two everyday guys forced to transform into superheroes. We would need magical powers, as our quest was to fight powerful monsters. The story featured surprise encounters with demons that didn't exist.

Or did they exist? What bubbled up was a tale that scrambled the ordinary so tightly with the bizarre that at times it was impossible to tell what was happening. The two of us were on a journey set inside Mike's favorite movie, a setting where those aboard were the only ones who did not understand how the story ended.

Pieces of the story drifted into my mind spiced with vivid bits of memories of the hours I had spent with him. No matter where this story was going to take us, Mike and I were not worried. We both knew that, in the end, every story we had ever shared in our adventure had worked out perfectly.

Each story started with four words, words that launched Mike and me into far-fetched realities. Those words held magic. They warned us we were about to fight monsters against enormous odds. Yet they assured us. We both knew that in every story we ever started with those four words—no matter what happened—the story would have a happy ending. And so this story began.

"Once Upon a Time . . ."

19

The Titanic: An Obsession

It was impossible to tell the precise moment when things started going haywire in Mike's mind. What the hell was normal behavior in a teenager anyway?

Life was confusing on the best of days. When puberty, independence, and naiveté about the world got thrown into the mix, all bets were off. At what point did behavior fueled by a creative imagination turn into actions directed by a mind that was starting to misfire? There was no clear delineation.

When that shift took place in my Little Brother, I will never know. My knowledge of Mike's daily life was limited to what I observed in the time we spent on outings each week. What I saw from him in our few hours together paled in comparison with the confusing (and alarming) actions Betty saw around their home. She would fill me in on some details, but I was insulated from most of his bizarre behavior.

In late 1998, another shift took place that changed our Big Brother matches. Joe and I sold our Seattle home and moved one hour south to Gig Harbor in Pierce County. The move took us out of the service area of Big Brothers of King County. As a result, the agency closed our matches.

Both Joe and I told the moms and our Little Brothers we were willing to continue doing outings with the kids and spending time with them. The agency offered Mike and Nate the option of being re-matched with new volunteers, which they both declined, so Joe and I continued working with

Mike, Nate, and both their moms as their "unofficial" Big Brothers.

****

Titanic was a blockbuster hit that was released in theaters at the end of 1997, and Mike and I went to see it in early 1998. What I saw was three hours of Leonardo DiCaprio charming his way in and out of endless crises until—thankfully—he went down with the ship.

Mike experienced something much different. He didn't just watch *Titanic*, he stowed away on the ship. That film sent him cruising on a voyage that flooded our times together for over a year. Mike talked about the *Titanic* every time we were together. He was captivated by the ship, obsessed about what people did as it was sinking. He talked endlessly about Captain John Smith trying to hold the wheel as the ship sank.

"What would you do if you was Captain John Smith?" It was the same question he asked me at every outing for several months. Yet every time he asked, he waited for my answer.

"I don't know, Mike. I'd probably try to find out as much as I could about what was happening and see if I could put out a distress call as soon as possible."

"Where would you go if you was Jack?"

"I'd probably go up top and help get the lifeboats out."

"Oh. I would go to the very top and hang on."

Fear was never a passenger on Mike's *Titanic*. He had no comprehension of the panic, absolutely no sense of the horror that was felt by the folks on board. He was enthralled by the sinking, obsessed by the dazed look in the captain's eyes while he gripped the wheel as icy water engulfed the bridge.

But Mike's *Titanic* didn't sink when I dropped him off at the end of the day. It never stopped drifting into every corner of his imagination.

"Do you know what this is?" he asked when I arrived for one visit. The white paper in his hand had the crude drawing of a ship.

"The *Titanic*?"

It was an easy guess. The ink drawing was no different from any of the others he had drawn over and over the previous few weeks.

"Yeah. And this is where Captain John Smith went when they hit the ice."

THE TITANIC: AN OBSESSION

Mike filled sheet after sheet with line drawings of the *Titanic*. The most accurate ones were those he traced out of books. He often tried drawing freehand using a ruler and pen to sketch crude drawings of the ship's outline. Occasionally a drawing would show the *Titanic* afloat, but in most the ship was sinking at an angle or splitting apart. Every drawing included a smokestack, the detail identifying it as the *Titanic*.

It was impossible to throw Mike off the sinking ship. He wasn't just sailing on it, he was living there. Every time Mike and I got together the *Titanic* drifted into our discussions. I'd pick him up, then ask about what he had done since I saw him last.

"I been making drawings. The *Titanic*."

His questions would start anew.

"If you was Jack and Rose, where would you go when they hit?"

I would let him ramble on, trying to answer a few questions. Then I would try to change course.

"Let's talk about something else, Mike."

"Talk about what?"

Good question. There was nothing else that interested him. He was oblivious to anything happening around him. He was at sea, hopelessly adrift on the *Titanic*. The longer the *Titanic* sailed, the further the two of us moved away from any common ground.

****

Only one thing could distract Mike from his *Titanic* fixation. Video games. *House of the Dead* was his favorite at one arcade; *Mortal Kombat* ranked on top at another. I hated the games. My hand-eye coordination was given to someone else when I was born, and I was totally inept at shooting figures scampering around a screen.

My role was to feed quarters into the machines to keep Mike entertained. He became better and better at the games, making it cheaper to play for a long time. The flip side was that with his improved skill level, he could play forever. Watching him blast away at a screen bored me to death. When the supply of quarters would finally dry up, Mike would blast his way through the last game. Then he would stare at the screen before slowly backing away.

When he stopped, I tried to pull myself back from whatever mental vacation I had been on while he was shooting.

"Who was your favorite?"

"Huh?"

"Your favorite?"

"Character? My favorite character?"

"Yeah."

"Uh, I don't know, Mike." *My favorite was that handsome guy who had walked past the arcade while you were annihilating characters.* "I really don't know. How about you?"

"Jax."

Momentarily, we had come off the *Titanic*. We were now stuck in a martial arts tournament in the realm of *Outworld*. It was a different imaginary kingdom, but it was still an impossible place to carry on any type of conversation.

After our outing, I sketched our day on Mike's calendar. Betty watched from her easy chair as Mike snuggled beside me. Another sketch of the *Titanic* joined those sailing on a long fateful voyage across every page of the previous few months.

My drawings of the ship differed from Mike's many sketches. In mine the *Titanic* was still afloat, showing other people on the ship.

When I finished drawing, we examined the sketch, tiny stick figures of Mike and me aboard the *Titanic* sailing for weeks on end. We stood on the deck, watched the people and enjoyed the view. Together we cruised along, both of us oblivious that our journey had shifted course and was heading into dangerous, uncharted waters.

20

Escape From Children's Hospital

"Hi, Betty. What are you up to?"

"As little as possible."

It was the same way our conversation always started. I could picture Betty in her kitchen, sitting at a round table in the eating nook, looking out at the small brick enclosure in her front yard.

"I'm just calling to check if tomorrow still works for me to get together with Mike."

"Actually, Mike is up at Children's Hospital. I had to take him there yesterday, and they are having him stay for a while."

"What's wrong? Did he get hurt?"

"No. He's in the psychiatric part."

"The psychiatric ward?"

"Yes."

I didn't ask what happened. Something must have gone on at home, and Betty may have overreacted.

What I was hearing seemed so out of the blue, so extreme. I didn't ask for an explanation; it was not really my business, but I thought it was strange. While the news shocked me, deep inside something told me this should not be a surprise.

"Do you know how long he'll be there, Betty?"

"Not really. It just depends on how things go."

"Can he have visitors?"

"Yes, and he would probably like that. I'll give you the number . . ."

I heard her shuffling through the small stack of papers she kept near her kitchen table. I had seen her look through that collection many times, a pile of handwritten notes and phone numbers. It was her lifeline, the contact information of the people and agencies involved in her and Mike's lives, a lifeboat that helped her navigate the challenges of raising an adoptive son with disabilities.

****

There it was: the doorbell to Hell. Just a little intercom box mounted on the wall beside the door. Visitors came here, rang the bell, waited, and hoped for the best.

I didn't know what to expect, but I was surprised anyway. This was Seattle Children's Hospital, where the halls were decorated with pictures and toys. Happy decorations were carefully positioned at every turn, chosen to bring comfort, trying to assure folks that everything would be okay.

Yet near this particular door every wall was bare. There were no happy murals. No oversized teddy bears or Disney characters had ever ventured down this hall. Here I was standing alone right outside The Land of Imagination Gone Wild. I took deep breaths, trying to absorb that Mike was in there, and wondering why I was here. I pushed the buzzer, and a pleasant attendant opened the door.

"I'm here to see Michael. I'm Dennis, his Big Brother."

"Wait here." She smiled and waved me inside. "I will go get him."

The waiting area was a peaceful, well-kept border zone, a serene space between here and there. Thankfully, this was as far as I could go. Through small windows in the second set of doors, I saw people walking in the hallway.

My only exposure to mental health facilities had been watching *One Flew Over The Cuckoo's Nest.* That was the atmosphere I expected, a hospital with patients in bed, IV tubes and machines everywhere, filled with heavily sedated weirdos.

But this looked and felt more like an office. I didn't hear any screaming, there was no pounding on walls, no craziness gone wild. All I heard was the muffled sound of waiting, waiting for something to change, and waiting for answers that might never come.

A few minutes later Mike sauntered down the hall. He was wearing street clothes, shuffling along in the unhurried way he always walked. He didn't seem frantic, didn't seem a bit different.

Until he came through the doors of the ward; then I saw what was different. There was fear in his eyes. In the six years I had known him, this was the first time I had seen him afraid. I reached out and gave him a hug.

"How are you doing, Mike? I was sorry to hear that you are in the hospital."

"Yeah."

"What have you been doing since you got here?"

"I played some games and rested."

I had no clue what they were doing with him, no idea of what they were trying to work with. Mike didn't know either. He didn't know what was happening, didn't have a clue why he had landed in here. I tried to reassure him, tried to let him know it was all right.

"Want to play a game, Mike?"

"Okay."

We pulled a game out of the toy collection, then killed some time chattering about what we had done recently and what we might do the next time we went on an outing. His confusion didn't seem to subside, and neither did his fear.

"So, you are going to stay here for a couple days till things get a bit better I guess, Mike."

"But how come?"

"Betty said they will have you stay here for a little while so they can help you with some things so you will feel better."

"How long?"

"I don't know. Probably just until you feel better."

"Sometimes my mind plays tricks on me."

"That is what they can help you with. They can help you know when your mind is playing tricks and what to do. You keep working hard. It will be okay."

"I am trying. I try not to wash my hands too much. So they don't think I'm crazy."

I wanted to cry. The kid was fighting to control a compulsion to wash his hands, hoping the hospital staff wouldn't think he was crazy. Mike knew something was wrong, and he was trying like hell to do what he could to fix it.

As he stared at the game board, his words in that hotel room during our Disneyland trip floated into my mind. *"All I want is to be normal."* This was not Disneyland, this was much worse.

****

A few days after my visit with Mike, I called Betty to try find out why he was in the psych ward. Her answer surprised me.

"He what?"

"He walked out of Children's Hospital." Her voice was tired. "Apparently he was in a furniture store, resting. The employees were getting ready to close the store, and they found him hanging around."

"A furniture store?"

"That's right. By Southcenter Mall."

"Southcenter? Way down there near SeaTac airport?"

"Yes. Mike told them he was going to walk over the mountains and live there. He got tired and stopped to rest."

"He walked the whole way?" I couldn't believe what I was hearing.

"That is what he said," Betty said, recounting what Mike told her. "I can't believe he could just walk out of the hospital without anyone noticing or saying anything. The guy is . . .well, Mike is certainly no rocket scientist."

Betty was angry, and for good reason. This was Seattle Children's, one of the premiere hospitals in the Pacific Northwest. How did Mike, who just two days earlier was trying to act sane by not washing his hands, walk out of that place? How could he simply leave a locked ward, walk out the front door without anyone noticing, and walk twenty miles on his way to start a new life "over the mountains"?

"Where is he now?"

"They took him back to Children's Hospital. I think they are pretty nervous about having a patient walk away."

They should be nervous! Without a doubt, the hospital administrators were in for a piece of Betty's mind. Incompetence drove her crazy, especially after sacrificing so much to help Mike and keep him safe. When she entrusted him to the hospital, the least she expected was that they would keep him inside the building!

Southcenter. I hung up the phone, and visions of Mike plodding along all day filled my head. *Where did that plan come from? What the hell was he thinking, just walking off? At least he had the good sense to try to spend the night sleeping at a store that sold mattresses.*

Talk about a head-scratcher. None of it made any sense.

21

To Eat or Not to Eat

Mike was losing too much weight. Since the first day I met him, Mike had been a chubby kid. Not fat, not thin, just chubby. His shape was a good fit for the bull in a china shop way he moved. Slow, steady, just plowing along and smashing into anything in his way.

As Mike transitioned into his teenage years, he started to put on weight. He added some height, but the extra pounds became visible as his physical activities gave way to sitting at a computer playing games. I tried to keep some exercise as part of our outings to offset his decline in activity. Betty tried to watch his diet, but Mike didn't seem overly concerned about his weight.

A few months after Mike's stay at Children's Hospital, Betty caught him putting a knife into his backpack to take to school. That resulted in him being admitted into the psychiatric ward at Seattle's Harborview Hospital for evaluation. When he returned home after the week-long hospitalization, there was a change in his appearance. He was getting noticeably lighter.

"Mike, it looks like you are losing a little weight," I mentioned one afternoon.

"Uh, yeah. I, I don't want to be fat."

"You aren't fat, Mike."

"I am. I am getting fat. In—in my stomach and I want to be thin."

"It's okay to watch what you eat. But you are growing and it's not good to lose too much. Are you on a diet?"

"No."

"Well, I notice you lost some weight.

After a few seconds of silence, Mike spoke up.

"I learned how to not get fat."

"How?"

"I learned how not to get fat."

"Where did you learn that?"

"In the hospital. I was in the hospital and I learned not to get fat."

"They taught you how not to get fat?" I was puzzled. "In the hospital?"

"Yeah."

"What did they teach you?"

"There was a girl. Her teached me not to get fat."

"A hospital worker?"

"No."

"A nurse or someone?"

"No. A girl. A girl who was at the hospital. She tell me how not to get fat."

"What do you mean?"

"She tell me if you throw up after you eat, then you don't get fat."

"Uh, Mike, that is not good."

Dead silence.

"It's dangerous, Mike. You need the food. You need to digest it to help your body stay strong."

"Uh-huh. But I don't want to be fat."

"It is dangerous for you to throw up after you eat. Have you told Betty?"

"No."

"It's important that she knows so she can help you."

He reached out and turned up the radio.

"Mike?"

"I want to talk about something else," he retorted. "Do you like this song?"

Our discussion was over. He was bulimic, and I needed to talk to Betty privately.

She and I spoke the next day. She was worried because he was not eating much at home, but didn't know he was purging after eating.

"I've tried to talk to him, to let him know he needs nutrition," she said. "He just starts talking about some twin girls on TV. They're his age. Anytime we talk about eating, he brings them up. He is focused that they are his age and are much thinner than him."

It was getting harder and harder for Betty to find any rhyme or reasons for much of Mike's behavior. She wasn't alone. Joe, Nate, and I had all noticed that Mike was becoming more erratic. As weeks went by the changes in his eating habits became more pronounced. He would not eat when we went on our outings, he would simply reply that he wasn't hungry. I tried to challenge him.

"Are you sure you don't want anything Mike?"

"No."

"Have you eaten anything today?"

"Yes."

"What did you eat?"

"Breakfast."

"And what did you have for breakfast."

"Uh . . . Let's go to the park."

Betty continued to have trouble getting him to eat. Mike would flip any food conversations back to the TV twins.

"He keeps talking about them, about how they look thin. I don't know what he is thinking," she sighed. "I tell him they are girls, that he is a growing boy and needs to eat."

I started monitoring him, trying to encourage him and reminding him he needed to eat to stay healthy, but it was pointless. When he did eat, it was only small amounts of rice. He had gotten the idea that rice was healthy, and it was fine if that was all he ate. He continued to starve himself and purge after eating. The pudgy kid was quickly turning into a scrawny teenage skeleton.

****

"What a great day, Joe."

"No kidding," he said. "A perfect day to be out in the boat."

TO EAT OR NOT TO EAT

We were wrapping up a great summer afternoon of boating, tubing, and swimming on Puget Sound. Joe, Nate, Mike, and I had spent hours out on the water, enjoying an August day that was hot enough to make swimming in the cold water feel comfortable. As everyone was changing out of dripping clothes, a couple pizzas were in the oven for an early dinner.

"You about ready, Mike? We need to leave soon for the ferry."

"Yeah. Almost ready."

"What kind of pizza do you want?"

"I'm good."

"What?"

"No pizza. I'm good."

"You don't want any pizza?" It had always been one of his favorite foods.

"No, but thanks for asking."

"Do you want something else? A sandwich or something."

"No. I'm good."

The eating stalemate. It was like negotiating with a starving brick wall.

"Mike, you haven't eaten all day."

"I have some before."

"What did you eat before?"

"Mountain Dew. And some orange pop. I'm good."

"Mike, come on," Joe encouraged. "You have to have something to eat." Mike respected Joe. Maybe he could persuade him to eat something.

"No."

End of discussion.

Twenty minutes later Mike and I were on the highway. He was fiddling with the radio, flipping through channels to any station with loud electronically scrambled sounds pulsating to an obnoxious beat. It was an annoying closing to a relaxing day on the water. Suddenly he gasped.

"Ah, can you stop?"

I looked over. He was pale, his face contorted.

"Mike are you okay?"

"I, I, I . . ."

"Are you sick?"

BLAFF! He exploded like a volcano. Orange barf blasted out and splashed on the dashboard. Then a second eruption, a river of orange soda pushed by Mountain Dew exploded and cascaded all over the truck, all over Mike.

"I, I sorry . . ." Mike gasped.

As the loud music pulsated, Mike gagged, and vomit dripped off the dashboard. I held my breath and thought, *This is serious!*

22

Random Wanderings

"So where did you go, Mike?"
"I was by that-that building.
"The building?"
"Yeah, the building."
"Which building, Mike?"
"With the games. Where we go."
"At the University? The place where we go play pool at the University?"
"Yes. At . . . that one."

He was telling the truth, I was sure. We were walking aimlessly around Seattle's Queen Anne neighborhood on a magnificent spring day while he was on a pass from the Seattle Children's Home. Mike had been placed there after making serious threats toward Betty. It was not the first time his anger had been directed toward her, but it reached a breaking point.

"He was home playing on the computer," Betty told me. "I said it was time to turn it off. He stopped suddenly, glared at me, and got very angry."

"I could kill you," Mike snarled at her. Then he pointed to the crib where Betty's infant great-grandson Damian was sleeping.

"And I could kill him too!"

"The way he said it—I could tell he wasn't kidding. I've done everything I can. It is just not safe to have him here, for me or for the rest of our family."

****

The sunshine seemed to spotlight the colorful rhododendrons in full bloom in every yard we passed. The sunny day was so welcome after the dreary events that had recently transpired in Mike's life. Dressed in sweatpants, a dirty sweatshirt, and untied tennis shoes that flopped as he walked, Mike seemed relaxed. But his breathing was strained as he shuffled along. A recent adjustment to his medication regimen had ballooned his weight.

The pass to leave the group home campus was a life-saver. Indoor visits at the facility were miserable. The nonstop shouting and chaos inside the group home were awful distractions. Also, Mike now refused to bathe, and his smell was overwhelming. As we walked, Mike talked freely, and I tried to absorb every bit of information about his latest adventure.

"Where did you sleep?"

"At the building. And at Barnes and Noble."

"Did you stay there all night?"

"No. In the day. I sleep in the day."

"Where did you sleep at night, Mike?"

"At night I-I walk. I was scared to sleep. So I just keep walking."

"You walked all night?"

"Yeah."

It was hard to think of him walking all night, alone and afraid. As he talked, I tried to unravel the mystery of the three days he spent roaming around the University of Washington. Following a lengthy stay at the Children's Home when he was first removed from Betty's, Mike was transferred to a foster home on Mercer Island. Mike's social workers had hoped a foster situation might work better for him than a group home.

The new foster father had signed Mike up for a karate class. On the way to class, Mike ran away dressed in his white karate-gi with a yellow belt. Three days later, a local TV station broadcast a news report about a missing intellectually disabled kid last seen wearing a karate outfit. The manager of the University Village Barnes and Noble called the police and let them know Mike was hanging out there.

"Then you would sleep during the day?" I asked.

"I go there. And sleep in the building."

"Then when you weren't sleeping, where were you?"

"At the University."

"And what did you do at the University?"

"I was just blending in. I blended in."

Blending in? He had to be kidding. For three days he was roaming around town decked out in a karate outfit. *Just blending in? Just how many other 275-pound Ninjas were there walking aimlessly around the University of Washington? Blending in?*

"What about food? What did you do for food?" I inquired.

"I was at Seattle's Best Coffee at the store. And I got some food."

"Did someone give you food?"

"Them was having coffee, and when they was done there was food."

"They gave it to you?"

"No. They left."

"Leftovers? On their table?"

"Yeah. So I-I had food."

"You ate their leftovers?"

"Yeah."

I was afraid to ask the next question.

"Mike, did you steal anything from the store?"

"No. There was food. On the table."

The image of him scrounging leftovers disturbed me. At least he was able to survive without shoplifting. *As the gas fireplace flickers in the cozy confines of the Seattle's Best Coffee outlet, the Ninja lurks in the shadows. Quietly he watches, waiting and ready to pounce on the uneaten food.*

"Is that how you ate all the time?"

"Sometimes I go there and I get food. Once a guy let me eat some of his food."

"At Seattle's Best?"

"No. On the trail."

"The trail?"

"The trail. By Betty's. Him was homeless and him ask if I want some food."

"He shared his food with you?"

"I eat the food. But him was dirty and I was afraid I might get some germs. So I put soap in my mouth to wash."

"You put soap in your mouth to wash? After you ate?"

"Yeah. I put soap in my mouth. So I didn't get germs from dirty food."

It broke my heart. My buddy, the Ninja, sharing food with another poor soul out on the streets. Then filling his mouth with soap to kill the germs.

"You were at the bookstore when they found you?"

"Yeah. The police come and they found me."

"If the police didn't find you, how long were you going to stay away?"

"For some more days."

"How many days? A week or more?"

"Yeah. A week."

There was nothing I could say. Mike's options for living arrangements had narrowed drastically. This last episode of running off came only days after he had torn apart a bathroom at his foster home in a fit of rage. The foster father had finally given up. He was not willing to take Mike back after this violent episode.

I couldn't blame the foster father. Earlier that month, Joe and I had attended an informational meeting discussing guardianship for disabled adults. We were exploring options that might help Mike find stability in his life and were checking if one or both of us becoming his legal guardian might help him. We had ruled out having him live with us, knowing his erratic behavior required more intense supervision than we could provide.

The meeting covered the duties, responsibilities, and state laws that applied to guardianship. Our hope was that, as his guardians, we would be able to help Mike find and continue medical treatment for his illness. But we learned that state law required that any treatment or hospitalization he underwent needed his consent or a court order if he refused. The presentation also made it clear there was nothing that shielded the guardian from liability should Mike cause harm to people or property.

Joe and I decided becoming his guardian would do little to help Mike and would put us at risk. We decided to continue trying to help Mike the best way we could—by supporting him as solid friends. We were discouraged, knowing that Mike's future would likely be determined by his own out-of-control decision making.

So for the time being, Mike had once again landed back at the Seattle Children's Home. He was assigned to a wing for teenagers where "staying put" relied heavily on the honor system. Given his history, I doubted the arrangement would work for long.

Mike did not seem concerned about burning bridges. He didn't seem to understand that soon there would be no place for him to return after he ran away. All he knew was that running off eased his frustrations.

Yet maybe Mike did, in fact, know that the bridges were burning. He had been shuffled between living arrangements ever since his threats to kill Betty made it impossible for him to stay with her.

Why should he care if the bridges burned? He no longer had a "real" home. What difference would the next—or any—transition really make to Mike? No matter how he or anyone else tried to put the puzzle of Mike's life together, there was a problem. The pieces of the puzzle never fit.

23

Gone Again

"Dennis, this is Betty. Did the Children's Home call you?"

"No. What's up?"

"Mike just called them. He told them he was okay, that he was having a lot of fun. He said that he was going to be gone for another week or two so he can see how long he can stay away."

"Where was he calling from?"

"They didn't know."

"Did he call you?"

"No. Just the Children's Home. Said he was having a blast."

The fact that he had called was great news. It had taken less than two months for Mike to blow off the honor system at the Children's Home and run away. He had been missing without a trace for six days.

"Did they trace the call, Betty?"

"Not that I know of."

"I wonder if they can find out what number he called from. If they can get a phone number we might know what area to look for him."

"I'll call them back."

The lack of information about Mike had been getting more unsettling each day. His latest vanishing act was the first thing that popped in my mind every morning when I woke up. Joe and I talked about searching for him, but where would we even start to look? It had been two years since he walked out of Children's Hospital. That night, they found him twenty miles away. He planned to "walk over the mountains and live there." After missing for a week this time, Mike could be anywhere.

"Hey, Joe, the Children's Home phoned Betty to tell her Mike had called them."

"Are you kidding?"

"Nope. He said he was having a blast, said he was going to stay away, trying to see how long he could stay gone."

"Where was he?"

"They didn't know. All they did was call Betty."

The tone of my voice saved me the trouble of telling Joe I was really pissed at Mike. He was out having "a blast" while Betty was home worried sick. Joe didn't say a word. He knew that Mike was a hell of a lot goofier than I would ever admit.

Then suddenly it hit me.

"I bet he's at Seattle's Bumbershoot Festival!"

"What do you mean?"

"I bet he is hanging out at Bumbershoot, the art and music festival. He said he's having a blast. He likes going to Seattle Center, we go there all the time. This weekend it's packed with people. There's people, food, and a big arcade of video games. Plus, in a big crowd, nobody will notice him."

"You think so?"

"I'd bet anything on it."

****

On our way to Seattle Center that evening, Joe and I stopped at the Channel 13 television station. An interview had been set up for me to try to get exposure on the hunt for Mike.

"He has been missing for a week. From the Seattle Children's Home on Queen Anne," I stated.

"You are his Big Brother, correct?" the reporter asked.

"Yes. I was matched as his Big Brother when he was seven. He's developmentally delayed, which puts him at risk when he is out walking around."

I tried to answer her questions with sound bites that might get on the news. I was hoping they didn't know Mike had run away before. It was a fine line I was walking. *"Missing Disabled Boy"* was scheduled to be on the TV news that night. If they knew it was just *"Runaway Teenager,"* they would throw me out of the building.

"Do you have any idea where he might be?" she asked.

"I suspect he may be spending time in places he knows. His family is very concerned. They ask anyone who has seen him to call the police department."

I didn't bother to mention the fact Mike had called earlier in the day saying he was having a blast roaming the streets. All I cared about was that the information got on TV and that someone, somewhere would find Mike.

****

Seattle Center was busy despite the rain. By the time we arrived, the crowd had whittled down to die-hard Bumbershoot aficionados, a fringe breed of retro hippies. In our clean, conservative clothes, Joe and I stuck out like sore thumbs. As we walked through the crowds, we got the evil eye from everyone. We scanned their faces looking for Mike; they were sure we were cops and shot us looks telling us to get lost.

"You go look in the pavilion. I'll go check the video games. Call if you see him."

"All right," Joe replied. He was fired up for this fugitive-on-the-run adventure.

I took one step inside the arcade and recognized the pants. Dirt hid most of the white fabric, but the baggy style was a dead giveaway. This time Mike's karate pants did not let him blend in.

Thousands of people had roamed in and out of Seattle Center that weekend. Yet right in front of me, in the first place I looked, I found my Little Brother. He was busy shooting up *House of the Dead*, his favorite game in this arcade. His pants gave him away, but I didn't recognize any of the rest of his filthy clothing. His head was newly shaved. He looked like a homeless bum.

"He's here! Where are you?" My hands were shaking as I ran outside to call Joe.

"What?"

"He's in the video game building. Come out the door you went in. Hurry!"

"You sure?"

"It's him! Hurry or we'll lose him!"

"What do we do?" Joe asked as he ran up. "Want me to call 9-1-1?"

We watched as Mike continued blasting at the screen.

"No. We'll go up to him," I answered. "If he starts running, then call 911."

Mike was so focused on the game that he didn't notice us approaching. I moved up on his right side, Joe was on his left.

"I get the next game," I said. Mike looked over at me.

"No, I'm playing the next one," Joe hollered. Mike glanced at him, then back to the screen. He continued shooting.

"Oh shit!" Mike mumbled. "I'm caught."

24

Reflections on the Run

"You don't want anything?" Joe couldn't believe I was turning down a chance to eat.

"No." I couldn't eat if I'd wanted to. Mike's foul body odor was stinking up the truck. The stench was killing any appetite I had. I tried to stay as calm as I could.

"Where were you, Mike?" I asked.

"I was at the Sea-Seattle Center most times. First I didn't know where to go. So I keep walking."

He was unusually talkative.

"Then I meet the Golden Gardens group. Then they give me some money, so I have some money. I tell them I was eighteen, and they think I was eighteen. I sleep outside for one night, at Golden Gardens. Then this guy has a place where I can stay, so I go stay there."

"You stayed with him?"

"Uh-huh, with him."

"Where? At his house?"

"Well. Ah . . . yeah." he stopped to think. "Sort of."

"Sort of?" The thought of some guy inviting Mike home with him was alarming on so many levels.

"Yeah."

"Who was he, Mike?"

"A guy."

"And you stayed at his house?"

He didn't respond. A week without his medication had made Mike very chatty. His conversation was fluid, the answers came easily. He was surprisingly alert and everything he said made sense.

There were specific details, like where he stayed, that he was keeping to himself. It was obvious Mike enjoyed the freedom of the past week. He was proud he survived on his own. And the way he was talking, it was clear he fully intended to do it again.

It was hard to look at him. The filthy blue coat he wore and his sweatshirt were new acquisitions. Somewhere along the way he also picked up a blue duffel bag, which I assumed he stole. My curiosity had gotten the best of me, and I did look through it before we left the arcade where we found Mike. My hope was that the owner's identity might be inside. But all I found were scattered pieces of Mike's weeklong odyssey.

There was a spiral notebook with a few pages of rambling poetry in someone else's handwriting. The information sheet from a local shelter was tucked inside a brown pocket-sized New Testament. The phone number of the Seattle Children's Home he had run from was written on a ripped yellow note card, again in another person's handwriting. On the bottom of the bag, under a schedule of Bumbershoot performances, a smashed peanut butter and jelly sandwich was loosely wrapped in plastic.

The transformation in Mike during his week on the streets astonished me. He had his head shaved to avoid being found, but he wouldn't tell Joe or me who had done it. When I saw him two weeks earlier, he was a subdued teenager, a guy just happy to spend the afternoon tagging along to a movie. By this night, my Little Brother had morphed into a proud and confident street bum.

It didn't faze Mike that he had not bathed all week. As he spoke with Joe, I got a sense Mike felt he had finally found his niche. He was proud that he not only survived roaming Seattle's streets, but also that he had thrived. He finally discovered a place he blended in, where he could roam unnoticed among the loosely organized society of Seattle's homeless. He had found camaraderie with others who were hiding in plain sight, existing just beneath the radar of those of us who were afraid to look too closely.

I couldn't shake the sense that finding Mike tonight wasn't an accident. How did we locate him among the throngs of people roaming Bumbershoot? I believe we found Mike there—decked out in the full finery of a street person—for a specific reason. It sent a message, one that was echoing in my head: *Take a good look. This is the future, and you better get used to it.*

****

Forty-five minutes after we arrived at the Children's Home, the cops showed up. Mike's options for living arrangements had narrowed again. The police planned to take him to a juvenile housing facility and keep him there until somebody could figure out what to do with him next.

"You the guy?" the cop wearing glasses bellowed as he stepped into the room and stared right at Mike.

"Uh-huh," Mike responded quietly.

"What's the deal?" the cop barked. "They said you were a psycho. You don't look all that dangerous to me."

What a sucker punch! I felt so sorry for Mike, a troubled teen in the hands of a guy like that jerk. I didn't care if he was a policeman—any guy stupid enough to make that type of comment was a calloused fool.

Seeing Mike put in the back of the squad car was unsettling, but it was a relief. It helped to know someone knew where Mike was, that he wouldn't be running off tonight, and, most importantly, that he was safe.

"Wow." It was all Joe could say as we walked back to the truck.

"At least we know where he is," I sighed. "And Betty can finally sleep without wondering what happened to him."

"I hope so. Man, what a day."

Numbness. It filled our truck the hour it took to drive home. We were buzzing down the freeway with the windows open but the awful smell of Mike's week on the street still hung in the air. Joe and I stared straight ahead, lost in thought. It had been a powerful night. The episode hit me as hard as anything I ever experienced.

"That was bizarre," Joe finally said.

"What part?"

"The whole thing. I can't believe we found him."

"Me either. And I don't think it was an accident."

"Neither do I."

That night we both got a clear glimpse of the road ahead. What we saw was surreal, and it was frightening.

Numb. There was no other way to describe it. My soul, my spirit, my entire body. I was completely numb.

25

... And Then God Sent Mike

One Afternoon in 1995

"You do-don't know what I have," Mike said, looking straight ahead as we drove down the street. His hand was resting just below the front pocket of his nice clean blue jeans. One quick glance and I could easily tell he had coins in his pocket, so many that it was bulging.

"It looks like you have some money, Mike," I said. I could never quite figure out this ten-year-old kid, and I was trying to stay one step ahead of him. "Did you take that out of your jar?"

Mike nodded. His jar was a quart glass container sitting on top of a cabinet high above the sink in Betty's kitchen. She had pointed it out to me two weeks ago, a growing slush fund that Mike earned doing chores. The money was going to be used for some special occasion when Mike would treat me on our outing.

This was the first time in our years as Big and Little Brothers that Mike was carrying money. Betty always gave me any money he was taking along, but for some reason on this day Mike had a stash of his own. It didn't take long to add two and two together and understand how it equaled a pocket full of coins.

When it was time to end our last outing, I'd told Mike I wasn't going to spend any more money on video games. He must have assumed that I meant I would never pay for any more. So the money sitting on the kitchen shelf became a perfect solution to what he saw as a huge problem.

"Did you ask your mom if you could take the money, Mike?"

"No," Mike mumbled. He fell silent and pondered how to handle this problem.

"Well, I think it's a good idea to talk it over with Betty before you take money or anything else out of the house."

"But . . .but it's my money," he stressed. It was a day when Mike had to work hard to get his mouth and mind working in unison. "It's mine!"

"I know. But it's a good idea to ask Betty before you take anything from the house," I repeated. "Let's make a deal. We won't spend the money today, and when we get home we'll ask Betty if it's okay to use it. If your mom says it's okay, we'll spend it next week."

The wheels spun in Mike's head, hoping to find a way to get me to let him burn the money now.

"Can we call her and ask?" he suggested.

"What if she says no? What if she says that you shouldn't have taken the money and she tells us to come right home?"

Mike sighed, knowing that was a real possibility. Slowly he resigned himself to the fact he wasn't going to be spending the money on this outing. I didn't say a word, giving him time to work through the issue.

"I didn't know about if I should take the money," Mike finally said. "So I prayed about it to God."

"What?"

"I was thinking about the money. Then I prayed to God about if I should take it."

"You prayed about the money?"

"Yeah, I pray about the money."

"About if you should take the money out of your jar?" I asked. He sounded serious.

"I didn't know about if I should. So I was praying if I should take the money. And then Betty went outside, and God said—" Mike lowered his voice, then shouted, *"TAKE THE MONEY! TAKE THE MONEY!"*

The car swerved as I doubled over with laughter. Mike seemed so innocent, like he actually believed God came to him right there in the kitchen. God arrived at the perfect moment as Betty stepped outdoors, and gave Mike the "Almighty Okay" to grab money out of his jar. God's will not withstanding, I knew Betty wouldn't be amused when she heard about the stunt later this afternoon.

While that was the first time Mike had shown up with money, it wasn't the first time God had been a topic of our conversations. Nor would it be the last time that God talked to Mike.

****

I used to have a solid idea of who God was, of what I believed about God. I knew how God operated, and my belief system wasn't something I questioned as I went about my daily life.

My concept of God formed early and was reinforced by my Catholic upbringing. It was a solid, drab mosaic of the tiny chips of morality I picked up from my parents and my Catholic school education. I glued the colorless design together as a kid as I watched and listened to what was going on around me.

From that point forward, I didn't question the foundation of my spiritual beliefs. I just accepted it as correct. My beliefs included a sense that God was present in my life through people around me. I might encounter someone by chance, only to discover that some part of our interaction gave me a flicker of spiritual understanding, a tidbit of insight to help guide me in my life.

And then God sent Mike.

****

"Him is this big guy up in the sky. He has magical powers," Mike declared.

Several months had passed since God told Mike to "Take The Money!" yet once again the two of us were discussing God. In fact, God had become a frequent topic during our outings.

"Magical powers? What kind of magical powers, Mike?"

"Him has magical powers. I pray to Him and he helped me."

"Like what? How did God help you?"

"Sometimes I pray to God and Him help me with my math homework," Mike explained. "And one time I was in the bathroom. I pray to God and

Him fixed the toilet before Betty finds out."

"He fixed the toilet? What, did it plug or something?"

"It plugged. So I pray to God. And Him fixed the toilet."

There it was, Mike's vision of God. Straightforward and simple. A Big Guy in the sky, sitting in the clouds with a calculator in one hand, a plunger in the other. Just waiting for Mike or anyone else to call on Him for advice on spiritual matters, algebra, or plumbing. Not a bad guy to have hanging around when you need him.

As absurd as Mike's vision of God seemed when he shared it, events in my own life had shown me that my perception of God wasn't much different than Mike's. My God was also a Big Guy in the sky, available to call on in times of crisis but was best left alone, because He was always watching, always monitoring.

My God also had a calculator, but wasn't doing algebra. He was watching me like a hawk and keeping score every time I screwed up. God was adding it all up, and little by little He was getting pissed. Sooner or later God was going to say He had seen enough, and whack me over the head with His plunger, and I'd be on my way to Hell for my sins.

A year and a half after I met Mike, my own struggles around accepting myself as a gay man reached a point where I needed help. I sought treatment for addiction and began the lifelong journey of recovery. Mike didn't know about this, but I did tell Betty. I told her that if she felt the Big Brother agency should know I was in addiction recovery, then I would tell them, but she and her family felt that wasn't necessary.

In the process of my recovery, I realized that my picture of God was a heavy mural I had hauled around since childhood. It was one I cemented together without ever asking if the pieces were real.

Here I was struggling to stay sober, yet believing in a God who was keeping score on my behavior. How would I ever get healthy, how could I expect to find any peace as long as I believed that God was busy adding up my shortcomings? I could look at people around me and understand that God had created each of them exactly as He wanted them to be. Why did I continue to believe that God had made a mistake when He created me?

I believe this is one reason God sent Mike. My talks with him were the first time in my life that I had to think about and explain, in very simple terms, what I believed about God. It helped me see that I needed to take a long, hard look at the spiritual force that was guiding my life.

****

An Afternoon in 2002

"You and those darn horses!" I told Mike, and he chuckled as he waited for me to make my move. Mike had just captured my queen with one of his knights and was moving quickly to beat me in another game of chess.

It was a fabulous September afternoon, sunny with temperatures in the mid-sixties. Mike and I were on the grass in the courtyard of the Seattle Children's Home where he was once again residing. I was thankful we were outside today, free of the confines of the stark, locked rooms that were now Mike's home. On the opposite side of the courtyard the home's other teenage residents tossed a football and profanity back and forth.

I looked over at Mike and tried not to feel discouraged. I struggled not to cry while we were playing chess. He was sixteen years old and had once again started hearing God's voice. In Mike's head, God's voice was blurred among too many others, and God was commanding him to do things. Mike inherited his biological mother's schizophrenia, and it was gradually strengthening its grip.

Recently God told Mike that water was dangerous, that something bad would happen if he got too wet. So Mike refused to bathe.

It broke my heart to see my Little Brother sitting on the lawn dressed in his stinky, ripped clothing. His navy-blue nylon pants were smeared with dried white goop, undissolved laundry detergent left from the last time he tried his hand at self-sufficiency. His hair was a tangled mess of unwashed black curls. He hadn't cut his hair since last year when he ran away from this group home and chopped all his hair off, trying to avoid discovery as he roamed Seattle's streets with other homeless people.

Mike was not allowed to wear shoes since an episode two weeks earlier when he ran off again. That time the police found him standing on Seattle's Aurora Avenue Bridge, threatening to jump off. So the group home staff kept him in stocking feet, hoping it would discourage him from running again.

Mike didn't say much anymore. The array of anti psychotic medications that quieted the voices in his mind stole most of his own voice too. On our visits, I looked at Mike and tried to accept what was happening, because I couldn't change his life; I had absolutely no control over whatever God had planned for him.

Whenever I went to see Mike, I asked God for guidance, for some help as Mike's friend. If it was God's will then maybe, *just maybe,* our time together would give Mike a few hours to feel free from the hell he was trapped in.

After my visits, when all the chess pieces and Mike were once again locked safely away, I cried. I sobbed so deeply because it hurt so much to see this innocent kid God sent into my life trapped in such torment. Amid my tears I prayed for Mike and begged God to please, please help my precious young friend.

I would ask God for the faith I needed to accept that the twisted state of Mike's mind really was, in fact, a piece of God's handiwork and not some huge mistake. I needed that faith. I was struggling desperately to understand why the child who helped me find my own God had been given such a heavy burden. Week after week I saw Mike slip a little deeper into the hell of mental illness. That filled me with anger and hopelessness because I knew I could not help him.

After these visits there were no more tiny stick figures on a calendar celebrating Mike's triumphs in our chess games. When our time together ended, there were only tears.

I would cry and pray. I would ask God to watch over Mike, to keep him safe. I would ask for His help to keep me sober and to guide me through the pain of watching Mike deteriorate. And as I cried myself to sleep at night, I would thank God from the bottom of my heart for that sacred day nine years earlier when He sent Mike into my life.

26

The Little Green Group Home

January 2004

It was not a bad place. The green house was no different from any of the other ramblers in this middle-class suburb of north Seattle. If I didn't know it was a group home, I would have never guessed by looking.

It seemed like an ideal place for Mike. It was a house, a far cry from the institutional atmosphere of the Children's Home that he had been bouncing in and out of for two years. It was a formidable challenge for Mike's case workers to find a suitable placement for him when he reached his eighteenth birthday. From my perspective, Mike had scored with this arrangement.

A residence for three other residents and staffed by a young laid-back crew, it felt like an actual home. Would Mike ever get to a point where he'd feel that this was where he belonged? Would he be able to find something that resembled a normal life? If that was ever going to happen for him, this place seemed comfortable enough to make it possible.

This weekend Mike was restricted to staying on-site due to arguing with staff members. I took it as a sign he was still having trouble making the transition into a new living situation. He could have a visitor, so my plan was to hang out at the group home with him for a few hours.

When I heard he was restricted to staying on-site, I didn't ask why. Client confidentiality prevented them from telling me; common sense kept me from wanting to know the details of the hell he was raising. During his first week staying here, Mike overdosed on medication he had been hoarding. He landed in the hospital, unconscious for three days. Seeing him lying in that hospital bed was crushing.

To my surprise he survived. He eventually came to and recovered surprisingly well. He showed no obvious signs of physical damage. However, the event added another scary edge to the ever-present cloud of volatile, dark energy that plagued him.

A loud alarm beeped when a male staff member opened the door.

"Hi, I'm Dennis, Mike's Big Brother."

"Come on in. Mike is in his room."

Eddie, a resident with Down syndrome, barely looked up from the living room couch. He was busy watching the Seattle Seahawks in a playoff game.

"Maybe, if you want, you guys can hang in here," the staff member said as he pointed toward Mike's closed bedroom door. "I think Mike will want to play video games."

He knocked on the door, and I could hear Mike shuffling toward us. Another alarm bleated when Mike opened his door.

"Hey, Mike, you have a visitor."

"Thanks." His tone was flat.

"Hi, Mike." I reached out and gave him a hug. He greeted me with a faint smile and a strong blast of body odor. I gritted my teeth, followed him into his room and heard the door shut behind us. Mike sauntered back to his desk, plopped into his chair, and grabbed the game controller.

"What are you playing?"

"This game," he replied. Without making eye contact, Mike resumed blasting away at characters scurrying about the screen. "Wanna play?"

"No thanks, I'll just watch you. What have you been up to, Mike?"

"Playing games. And I rest."

"Do you like it here?"

"Uh. Uh, yeah."

My barrage of questions was no match for the action on the screen. As Mike continued firing, I glanced around the room. His bed was roughly made, the only sign of order. Clothing, papers, and video game guidebooks were scattered wildly about. Dirty laundry cascaded out of a partially open closet door. The computer monitor took up the surface of his desk.

As the shooting dragged on, I heard vibrations when the forced air furnace whirred to life. Within seconds, the putrid stench of urine blasted out from the heat vent on the floor. I tried not to gag; Mike continued blasting away at the video game.

"Mike. Let's go watch the football game." I was choking in here.

"Huh?"

"Come on. We'll go watch the Seahawks. You can play this later." Before he could object, I yanked the bedroom door open and gasped for air. "Let's go."

Mike looked at the screen longingly, then pushed his chair back with a big sigh and followed me into the living room. Eddie turned away from the TV to stare at us.

"Can we join you?"

"Yes." Eddie smiled and pointed to a chair.

"Are you a Seahawks fan?"

"Yes! I like the Seahawks!"

Eddie also liked having company to watch the game. Mike, Eddie, and I made small talk and yelled at the refs and players on the TV. The Seahawks and Packers battled back and forth, and the contest went into overtime. The Hawks won the coin toss and elected to receive. Quarterback Matt Hasselbeck confidently announced to the world that the Hawks were "going to score" and win the game.

Then the Seahawks fell flat. They lost. Their season was over.

"Wanna play some video games now?" Mike asked.

"No thanks, Mike. I am going to head home."

"Okay. Thanks for coming here."

We shared our handshake, I said goodbye to Eddie, and Mike shuffled back to his room. The staff member came to let me out.

"Hey, Mike's room reeked of urine when the heat came on," I told him. "I think he's been peeing into the heat vent."

"Oh, thanks for letting me know," he sighed. "We'll check into it. We've

THE LITTLE GREEN GROUP HOME

been trying to work with him on a few things." The staff member didn't seem at all surprised.

****

My first visit to the green group home also turned out to be my last. Later that week I called Betty to check in.

"He's not there anymore. They kicked him out," she told me.

"Kicked him out?"

"Yes. Apparently, he put bleach or detergent into the milk in the refrigerator. He was trying to make someone get sick."

"Where is he now?"

"I'm not sure. They are trying to find someplace to keep him."

Someplace to keep him. A place where he was safe and where the people around him would also be safe. *Was that even possible?* Every time his caseworkers looked for available housing, workable options became fewer and fewer.

All these housing transitions made it much harder for me to keep track of him. His caseworkers would notify Betty when he was assigned housing, but her failing memory rarely caught the details of his placements. She would pass along a name or a phone number, and I'd have to track him down. On rare occasions, Mike would call me to tell me where he was. Then I would do what I could to arrange a visit.

The days of wrapping up a visit drawing stick figures were long past. Every time Mike was moved to a new living situation, more of his belongings were disposed of or just disappeared. The calendars with the stick figures that recorded our outings for the first several years were lost during Betty's move from her home in Queen Anne to North Seattle.

Several months after he was kicked out of the green group home, Mike was placed in a group residence in Covington in south King County. In contrast to the Seattle home, the place looked rough from the outside. The one-level house had an overgrown yard, visible deferred maintenance, and an aura that warned visitors to stay away. Large evergreens wrapped the building on three sides, casting shadows that kept the indoor living areas in perpetual darkness.

Mike and I went on one outing from the home, to a movie and then to McDonald's. When I walked him inside to sign him in after our outing, he quickly drifted through the dimness into his room.

A couple weeks after that visit, I called to schedule another outing. The staff told me that Mike had broken a TV. He was on restriction and could not have visitors or go off the property for at least a week. I opted out, having no desire to hang around inside that dreary house.

Two weeks later I called to see what Mike's status was for going on an outing. The staff told me he no longer lived there. They had no information on where he had been transferred, nor would they tell me why he was moved. Once again, the search was on for someplace to keep him. Someplace where he would be safe and where the people around him would be safe. Would they find a place?

Did such a place even exist?

IV

Hospitals

It is courage, it is foolishness, it is faith.
Sometimes there's no difference between the three.
Leonard Pitts Jr.

27

The Visiting Hours

"Okay, I'll let you go up."

I put the *People* magazine down and walked toward the reception desk. The guy with the shaved head stood up and took a break from clicking away at his computer. His indifference tonight was the same reaction I got every visit. I would sign in, tell him who I was here to visit, then sit and wait. He would dial the ward, tell them I was here, then continue to play video games and pretend he was busy.

After a return call, Mr. Excitement would tell me I could go up. He slid in a key and the elevator started churning. He didn't say another word. My guess was that he was wondering why anyone was foolish enough to come visit anyone who needed to be locked inside. I couldn't blame him for thinking that, because I was struggling with that question myself.

The elevator door slid shut, and during the fifteen-second ride I would pray: *"God, give me some guidance. Please help make this a good visit for Mike. Your will, not mine, be done."*

When the elevator door opened, I came face-to-face with God's will. On this evening, His will was scattered throughout the hall in people wearing blue and white pajamas. The first order of business was always to figure out who was who. It was a defense mechanism; sorting it out seemed to calm me down.

My first visit to this hospital was on Halloween. A monk in a brown robe was at the reception desk. When I stepped out of the elevator onto the ward that night, a flurry of people were moving about. It was impossible to tell the employees from the patients. I approached a slender woman with long hair and claw-like fingernails sitting behind a window at the nurses' station.

"Hi. I'm here to visit Michael."

"Sign in here." His deep bass voice boomed as he gave me a seductive smile. *Was it Trick or Treat? Who the hell could possibly tell?*

A few seconds later, Mike appeared. Since he arrived at this psychiatric hospital in West Seattle, he had been spending his days walking compulsively. That first night we walked up and down the hall, shuffling fifty feet in one direction, then turning around and walking back. As Mike strolled along in his slippers, I tried to make conversation and not stare at the other patients.

"Hey, Mike. The guy behind the desk by the elevator. Is his hair always that long, or is he wearing a wig?"

Mike stopped, turned his head, and stared at me.

"That's a woman," he said bluntly, then continued walking.

"Oh." We strolled on in silence.

Then Mike stopped abruptly. He leaned over and whispered, "You know, there's been talk about that."

****

On another visit, Mike was waiting for me at the elevator, holding the box containing his wooden chessboard. He was dressed in the same short-sleeved green shirt and khaki shorts he had been wearing for the last month. I walked over and gave him a hug. *He doesn't stink too bad tonight.*

"Hi. Good to see you," he said. His tone was a low, flat monotone. "What color do you want?" I asked as we settled at a table for our chess game.

"I gonna be . . .That one." He pointed to the white chess pieces. It was easier to point than talk. The medications they prescribed to help silence his mind had done a number on his voice too. For the first time I could remember, he chose the white pieces. Before that night, he always selected black. *What was up with that? Why the change?*

"I thought you liked using the black ones, Mike. Why did you change?"

"I change. That's my how-come," he mumbled.

THE VISITING HOURS

My how-come. It was the phrase that Mike started using to explain his reasons for behaviors or any decision he made. "My how-come" was his simple answer for all of the complex mysteries that swirled deep within him.

"Have you had any visitors, Mike?" Although he rarely got any, I asked him every time.

"Uh yeah."

"Who?" I asked.

"My workers." He stared at the chessboard.

"Your case-worker? Your attorney?"

"Uh—huh."

"Which one? The attorney or case worker?"

"My. Yeah. My case. The worker."

"What's their name?"

There was a long pause, then he looked up.

"I don't know."

Mike wasn't a gold mine of information. He would throw out a couple nuggets of fact, then I was left trying to assemble a picture of what had happened since my last visit. No matter how I put the pieces together, it always resembled just an existence, not a life.

"Remember my sister Peggy?"

"Uh-huh," he nodded, looking back down at the board.

"She's flying through Seattle tonight, so I'm going to go see her on my way home. She was in California for the weekend."

"That's good."

He didn't seem to care what I said. Hell, I didn't care either. We had very little to talk about. I tried to scrape together anything that might connect parts of our past. After months of being in this hospital, Mike's connections between yesterday and today were vanishing. Yet I kept on yakking while Mike stared at the board.

When he reached for a chess piece, his sleeve slid up and exposed the scars that covered the cuts he made on both arms a few weeks earlier. He had sliced himself up with sharp plastic from a broken light fixture. After smashing the light, he hid the piece of plastic in his room until he needed it.

"I had the piece in the shower. I think about the girl," he confided during my last visit.

"Then I knowed that I was going to cut with it. I thinked that it would be her or me. I didn't want to hurt her. So I cut me."

That was it, Mike's how-come.

****

On a later visit, we sat on plastic chairs on either side of a six-foot table. The Formica top was stained with paint from art projects. The room was decorated with patients' drawings taped to the wall. Some resembled the video game creatures Mike once enjoyed drawing, but none had his rainbow of colors. Before I could ask about the art, Mike had the chessboard set up and was ready to play.

"You're the champ Mike, so you go first."

He smiled when I acknowledged his skills. We had been playing chess in this hospital for over a year. I could count on one hand the number of games I won. *You'd think I'd be able to win at least one game of chess in the psych ward.*

Mike started with one of his usual opening moves of jumping a knight over the line of pawns. As I pondered my move, two guys entered the art room and sat down.

"I WOONA GA HOOOOMEE!" The sound rose from deep in the younger man's throat, more like a moan than speech.

"We'll have to see what the judge says, Max," his dad responded.

They were sitting at an identical table on the opposite side of the room. The father had brought his son, an adult patient, a pizza to share for dinner.

"HOOMME. I WOONA GO HOOOOMEE!" Max repeated.

"I know. Have you been good today?"

"YHAAA. YHAAA."

"Good boy. You keep doing that, and we'll see what the judge says. Here, have some pizza." Dad was doing his best.

As Mike contemplated his next move, I listened to Max and his father. I felt sick. There was no way in hell Max was going home. How could his family possibly take care of him?

Mike finally made a move. Without thinking, I moved a pawn, then sat back and listened.

"Here, son, have some pizza."

"I LIIIKK PPZZA."

It was obvious the man really cared for his son, enough to come visit him, enough to bring him dinner. The father talked, trying to engage his son. What did it feel like to see your own child here? How did it feel for a parent to see their own flesh and blood so badly damaged that he had to be kept locked away?

It was horrifying to imagine and was tragic to see. It was impossible to visit here and not feel an emotional jolt. I tried to focus on the chess board, but no matter where I looked—at the pieces, at Mike, or anywhere around the room—all the options seemed very, very bleak.

28

Wrestling Inside

"Sorry, guys; you'll have to move. We need the room."

A visitor with a baby had shown up, and the staff needed to provide a locked room for them. Unfortunately, Mike and I were in the only room available.

"No problem," I responded. Mike and I packed up the chessboard and headed into the noisy hall to find another room. *Who would ever bring a baby into this place?*

We entered the dining room as three patients got up to leave. I watched Mike to see if bouncing between rooms was agitating him. Not yet. Mike and I sat by a window and set up for another game. Our chessboard caught small strands of light that trickled in through the metal mesh on the exterior, creating a cage out of every window.

"Okay Mike, let's start over."

It was 6:35. Another twenty-five minutes and I could leave. Two hours was my limit. Mike and I ran out of things to talk about after the first few minutes. After an hour, I ran out of patience for getting whooped in chess. The remaining time was just that—time. Some visits were relaxed and as comfortable as the fit of a familiar sweatshirt. But on this night, time was dragging.

Why was I here? Why did I come visit Mike? Was I crazy for showing up every couple of weeks?

For some reason I was drawn here, to see for myself what shape Mike was in. I needed to see him physically, to try to sort out what had taken place since I last saw him. Whenever I drove toward the hospital, my gut would tighten up. There was never a nice surprise waiting when that elevator door slid open.

Mike had tried to kill himself several times the past couple of years. The poor guy was trapped inside a defective body. He was locked up to try to keep him from hurting himself. Or, as Joe so often reminded me, to try to stop him from hurting someone else. Would I blame Mike if he did kill himself? How long could he last like this?

From the glaring fluorescent lights of the psychiatric ward, my thoughts drifted back to the peaceful darkness of a California hotel room.

"I have a-a Lucky Life," the excited twelve-year-old Mike had told me. "I'm lucky! I got a good mom; I got Jake, my dog. I got you and my house. I got a Lucky Life!"

A Lucky Life. Maybe it was the wire mesh over the windows. Maybe it was that daze I saw in the eyes of patients whenever I mustered enough courage to look directly at them. Something was blocking the view. Inside the locked psychiatric wards playing chess, anywhere I looked it was impossible to catch even a glimpse of a Lucky Life.

****

There were voices outside. It was smoke break. Whether they smoked or not, the patients lined up early for the chance to go stand outdoors. They smoked in a caged area wrapped by a tall chain-link fence. Twice a day they gathered for fifteen minutes of freedom in a human kennel.

"I'll close the door," a strong male voice behind me hollered.

I turned around and saw the door slam behind them. *Damn!* Mike and I were suddenly alone in a closed room with two other patients. There was a tall slender guy in street clothes. Behind him, in pajamas, shuffled a clean shaven Max.

"AAHGGHAHH!"

Mike looked up from the chessboard and glared.

"Whose move now, Mike?"

The two guys walked toward a window several feet behind Mike. They stared outside. *What the hell am I doing? I'm sitting in a closed room with just the patients and me.*

"Hear that?" the thin guy yelled. "Hear that? There's a fight!"

"AAH-GGH-AHH." Max sounded like he was trying to laugh.

I couldn't hear any fighting. The only sounds outside were patients talking in the smoking kennel.

"Man, there's going to be trouble! Here come the cops!" the thin guy bellowed. "I hear a helicopter. Man, the cops are coming in a helicopter!"

I listened. No helicopter. No fighting, no yelling. Nothing. *What if one of these guys tries something?*

"Oh boy, I'm glad I'm not out there when the cops show up!" the thin guy exclaimed.

Suddenly Max started shuffling toward us, his uncombed sandy brown hair sticking out wildly. He couldn't close his mouth completely. There was a large gap between his front teeth, and he was drooling. Inside his glazed eyes an intense focus burned.

Mike darted him a warning look. The burly guy in blue pajamas and slippers kept coming. Max plopped down in a chair near Mike, then started kicking the side of Mike's chair.

"HHAANNANNA."

"Hey, knock it off!" I said. "Does that bother you Mike?"

The kicks got stronger.

"Uh-huh. How about you?"

"I'll get someone, Mike. Wait here," I said. Max kept smacking the side of Mike's chair as I jumped up.

"That's good," Mike growled. He stared at Max as the kicks kept coming.

"The cops still aren't here! I'm glad I'm not gonna be out there when they show up. Those guys are so screwed!"

I wished the damn cops would hurry up. For the first time on any of my hospital visits, I felt Mike and I were in a situation where violence was a real possibility. *Just fly the damn helicopter right through the caged window and restore order to our chess game.*

WRESTLING INSIDE

Dazed wanderers filled the hallway. One face stood out, a woman who wore an expression of calm authority. Before I had time to explain, she was herding Max and his buddy out of the dining room.

"That made me nervous, Mike. I didn't know what they were going to do."

"Uh-huh. My move?"

When I lost my last bishop, my luck turned from bad to worse.

"HUUHAAI!"

We had company again: Max. *I started shaking. Damn him! This sucks! I'm outta here!*

"Hey, Mike, let's call it a night."

He looked up, surprised.

"I can't concentrate, Mike. I'm leaving now." Mike was bewildered because our two hours weren't up. I didn't care. I'd had enough.

We shared our Big Brother handshake and a hug. I told Mike I loved him, and I tried not to look too excited when the elevator finally arrived, carrying me to freedom.

****

When I reached my truck I was still shaking. Fear and sadness were all stirring together inside me. Being inside that hospital hanging out in a locked world was stressful to say the least.

It was hard to believe that the sweet kid I met eleven years ago lived in chaos behind those locked doors. My buddy, a guy whose simple wish was to be normal, had grown into a confused, mentally ill man with a short fuse. Once lit, that fuse turned him into a monster.

But something still pulled me to visit Mike. What did I get by spending time in a place where people were locked away for safekeeping? Did I feel superior, better by comparison? It was a place to spend time with Mike, to play chess and try to connect with him. But it was a psych ward, a dangerous environment. Was I attracted by that?

When I left, I would wonder, *Was any of what I saw there really God's will? What would eventually happen to all the innocent folks locked inside, wandering aimlessly about, hurting, hoping, wanting to go home?*

Did I come here for Mike, or was it for me? Did that even matter? I knew

I showed up to let Mike know I was still there. I wanted to let him know that despite all that had happened, he still had a friend.

Just to see him, that was why I came. I needed to look into his eyes, see what was there, and to try to understand.

For me, visiting hours were a sacred time, where I learned to accept that I would never understand God's will for Mike, and that I could never, ever be able to change it.

Most important, it was during those precious hours we shared that Mike gave me the gift of insight. He showed me that unlike him, God had truly blessed me with a very Lucky Life.

29

Wedding Bells

It was a quiet, carefree evening at home just hanging out with Joe. As I finished washing the dishes, a call from a restricted number rang on my cell phone. It was probably Mike calling from the hospital to say hello and kill some time. The pattern of his calls to me was erratic, coming in bunches whenever he was bored.

"Hi, Mike, how are you doing tonight?"
"Good. I'm getting married!"
"What?"
"I am gonna get married."
"You are getting married? To who?"
"To a girl."
"A girl? Who?"
"A girl who is here."
"When, what—"
"Here, she wants to talk to you."

The sound of the phone shuffling between them was followed by rapid chatter from an excited female.

"Hi. Me and him are getting married! I think you have a nice brother. He is so nice and we are getting married. I like him and he wants to get married, so we are going to get married!"

When she paused to take a slight breath, I was able to barge in.

"That's nice. Can I talk to Mike again."

"Okay. Nice to talk with you. He is so nice. I like your brother." Then finally Mike's brand-new fiancée fumbled the phone back to him.

"Hey, Mike, who is she?"

"She is a girl who is here."

"And what made you decide to get married?"

"She ask me. She ask me if I want to get married. I said I want to get married. So we are getting married."

"When?"

"When we get out."

When they get out. That wasn't going to be anytime soon. But the way things happened in Mike's life, nothing was certain.

"Well, Mike, congratulations. I hope everything works out. I'll talk with you soon, okay."

"Yeah, bye."

Married—now that was a stunner. In all Mike's recent adventures, I never expected he would decide that! Especially to another patient in the psych ward. *And what if she gets pregnant?*

Joe saw how bewildered I was when I walked into the living room.

"What's up?"

"Guess who's getting married?"

"Who?"

"Mike. He called to tell me he was getting married and introduce me to his fiancée."

"Married? Mike? Married to who?"

"Another patient."

"You got to be kidding me!"

"I'm not. She asked him to get married. He says they're getting married when they get out."

"Well, that's not going to happen very soon," Joe chuckled.

"Probably not. But who knows?"

I rolled my eyes and took a deep breath. Then I looked over at Joe, my best friend and partner for the last twenty-five years.

WEDDING BELLS

"You know what's really crazy, Joe? Those two can legally get married. But you and I can't."

30

Our Chess Stadiums

Seattle Mental Health Hospital, 2004

A lady with dishwater-blond hair wearing shorts and a white blouse walked up to the table and introduced herself as Tina.
"I'm from California, and I'm just passing through."
"Nice to meet you, Tina."
"Is this your dad?" she asked Mike.
Mike looked up from the chessboard. "My brother."
"You're his brother?" She glanced from Mike to me and back as she tried to figure out why Mike was Native American and I wasn't.
"I'm his Big Brother, a friend," I explained.
"Oh. Well nice to meet you." Tina turned and strolled away. A short guy in his mid-twenties at the far end of our table sat watching, never saying a word.
"Let's see, is it my move?"
"Yeah," Mike mumbled.
Mike and I exchanged moves. Then without a word the short guy stood up and walked out of the room.
"Mike, does that bother you when he sits there?"
He pondered the question for a few seconds. "No."
Before I could move another piece, Tina returned. She didn't talk, just strolled across the room, turned around and walked out. She must have been

craving the warm California weather because she had on a sweater over her blouse.

Mike captured my second knight and then responded to my following move by capturing a bishop. The short guy returned and again sat at the end of the table. He started folding a long strand of toilet paper.

Mike glanced at him, then continued to contemplate the chessboard. He moved a bishop; I moved a pawn. Before my fingers were off the piece, Tina returned and walked toward the short guy. Her hair was now down, she had put on more mascara, and the sweater and blouse had given way to a halter top. For someone just passing through, she had a very extensive wardrobe.

"What are you doing?" she asked the short guy. He did not respond, didn't even look up from folding toilet paper. Tina shrugged and walked out.

"That's checkmate," Mike said flatly.

"Really?" I scanned the pieces.

"Good job, Mike."

"Wanna walk?" he asked.

It was time to leave the short guy to his folding and pace the hallway. We spent twenty minutes strolling together, up and down the hall, and going nowhere. When I finally stopped and told Mike I was leaving, Tina passed by wearing yet another change of clothes.

Western State Hospital, 2005

We were locked inside Washington's Western State Hospital. Before Mike was transferred here in the fall of 2005, just hearing the name Western State Hospital conjured up creepy thoughts of a mysterious, end-of-the-road institution where very serious cases were treated, even cases of criminal insanity. I'd dreaded even the possibility that Mike could end up here.

I was surprised what I found when I visited him here for the first time. It was modern and clean, and a definite improvement over the West Seattle facility where Mike had spent the previous eighteen months. The staff members were pleasant, and they treated both Mike and me with respect.

Mike and I played chess as the chaos of psychiatric ward life swirled outside our door. We were playing an ancient game in a place where, for decades, human beings had been kept locked up, like pawns on the chess board. There were some serious drawbacks to our game. The slop of leftovers on the table made me gag. My arm was fully extended trying to put some distance between me and the germ-infested scraps that I unceremoniously pitched into the waste basket, while Mike plopped down and started setting up the chessboard on greasy smudges of food.

"Hang on a second, Mike. Let me wipe that off."

"Okay," he sighed.

Today Mike and I were put into a utility room. The ward's visitor room was occupied, the dining room was being cleaned, and the weather was too cold to sit on the deck. So, we landed in the last available locked room that could be used for a personal visit.

Speaking of personal, the room held an intimate connection with every patient on this floor. As Mike and I set up the chessboard on a small table, I tried not to be distracted by the fact that tonight we would play surrounded by underwear.

Huge carts of industrial-sized blue bins crammed full of white underwear lined the wall behind me. Another one was pushed into a corner behind Mike. Still another was parked on the opposite side of the room. The bins were full of huge piles of white socks, white undershirts and tighty-whiteys of every imaginable size. On the window ledge beside our table sat stacks of clean underwear folded into piles.

It was impossible to tell if the underwear in the bins was dirty or clean, and I was afraid to look. The ever-present aroma of hospital disinfectant disguised whether the bins were heading to or from the laundry room.

Bright fluorescent lights were amplified by the reflection off all the white fabric. All the underwear created the same unsettled feeling that lurks in the darkness beyond campfire ghost stories. It was hard to shake the sense that something was about to jump out of the underwear pile and scare the hell out of us.

"My move?"

"Huh?" I was distracted by the underwear. "You are the champ, Mike. You go first."

He was not only the champ, but he was also playing on his home court. I was the visitor, locked in another strange arena to match wits over the chessboard. Focused on our game, I could almost forget where I was. On this ward, every room, every window, every exit was locked.

Just walking through the hospital door to come inside took grit and determination. I never knew what I would find inside, what condition Mike would be in when I visited.

Whenever I would take time to feel it, I was sick at heart. Here I was, inside a mental hospital surrounded by underwear and insanity because Mike could not function outside the locked doors. Unfortunately, psychiatric wards had become the setting for our chess games, Mike's home stadium. Game after game, week after week, we played. Chess was the only way we could share some time together. We competed while spectators walked aimlessly and occasionally stopped by to talk.

No matter where we played or who won the games, they always ended the same way. One of us went home; the other stayed locked inside, left behind to fend for himself among the unruly and confused. It bothered me immensely that my two dogs had more freedom than Mike and the other patients had here.

31

The Harry Potter Movie

11:30 am, December 8, 2005

It was December, but there was warmth swirling around inside me. This day felt special. For over eighteen months, Mike's existence had been limited to hospitals, on locked psychiatric wards. Somehow Mike had earned a pass for an afternoon out in the community. I was on my way to pick him up and take him out to lunch and a movie.

Would going out on passes become our new routine?

The thought was unsettling, but it was worth a try. Each time I visited Mike I noticed he had shriveled away just a bit more. His medications and his mundane existence were slowly destroying his interest in everything.

Maybe if Mike could get out in the world occasionally, it would help revive him. This outing was a chance to give him a breath of fresh air in the outside world. My hope was that maybe, just maybe, when he was on the outside, he would catch a glimpse of some hope. Maybe he would see something that would add a spark to his existence. If going on outings could pump some fresh life into his fading spirit, then the effort was worth it.

In the hospital parking lot, I heard a song on the radio about rain coming down on a sunny day. I shut off the engine. It was time to make the short walk up the stairs, ring the bell and get Mike. I took a breath to relax, and then double checked the door locks to make sure that no one hanging around would steal my truck.

THE HARRY POTTER MOVIE

"You need to be clean when we go out on a pass Mike," I had told him when we set up the outing. *Not too bad.* When he meandered down the hall toward me, it looked like he had at least tried to clean up. Mike still hated to bathe and wore the spilled remains of his last meal on the front of his sweatshirt.

The gray sweatshirt almost matched his dark green sweatpants. The pants rode high above his ankles, accentuating the tan socks that pulled my eyes down to his beat-up black tennis shoes. The Velcro straps were undone and his size 13 sneakers flopped as he shuffled toward me. *He looks like a mental patient.*

Mike's clothing was the perfect accessory to the hollow look in his eyes, those same eyes that once sparkled each time we'd meet. Once we were outside of this ward, I knew that Mike's look was going to make a very bold statement: *"Wow, there's something very, very wrong with that guy."*

The staff member slid two papers across the counter.

"Just sign here and you are ready to go. What time do you expect to be back?"

"We should be back by four."

The simple sign-out surprised me. I expected they would take Mike and me into a room and go over rules for the outing, but the woman behind the nurses' station just pointed to the papers and told me to sign. I scribbled my name to acknowledge that Mike was not the hospital's responsibility while we were out.

My expected list of rules, all the "dos and don'ts," never materialized. A simple "sign here" and then a pleasant blond woman escorted us to the door, unlocked it, and smiled.

"Have a nice day."

Off we went. In a matter of seconds, I was free to wander anywhere I chose with a guy who was kept behind tightly locked doors for nearly two years. Strange. Very strange indeed.

****

We went to get lunch before the movie. Mike struggled with the small foil ketchup packet for a few seconds before I offered to help.

"Want me to open that?"

"Yeah. Thanks."

His hands were shaking, his face devoid of expression. Mike's medications were a chemical straitjacket that continued to erode his muscular control, and turned his eyes into glazed, blackened windows. Here I was eating at Burger King with a medicated shell. Across from me was just a body that transported Mike, who was hiding somewhere deep inside, withdrawn into a fetal position.

My hope was that our time today would uncurl that position slightly. If we were lucky, maybe Mike would feel safe enough to look around. Maybe he would notice that the world was still turning outside the locked ward.

With every slow, jerking motion he made, my appetite faded. Mike's thick black hair was unkempt, filled with dandruff. Small flakes of skin fell from his face, Nature's confetti caused by his poor hygiene. Dressed in his sloppy, mismatched clothes, I knew he was struggling to function as best he could. I took a deep breath, bit my lip, and tried not to gag watching him eat.

****

A video game arcade just inside the theater lobby greeted us, strategically positioned to suck the last remaining cash out of patrons after they paid for movie tickets. Despite the musical whizzing and thumping sound of shots being fired on the game screens, Mike ignored the arcade, which was surprising. He had never passed any arcade without asking if we could "just take a look." A snack bar guarded the dark tunnel that led to the doors of the various theaters.

"Do you want anything to drink for the movie, Mike?"

"No. I'm good," he mumbled.

Harry Potter and his friends had grown up since Mike and I last saw them. The storyline was wrapped in a bizarre blend of magical images. We were deep into the film, and I was still totally confused by the story.

Mike sat to my left, his eyes glued to the screen. He hadn't reacted to anything on the screen since the film started. Suddenly he leaned over toward me.

"I have to go to the bathroom," he whispered. "I'll be right back."

Should I follow him? By the time Mike shuffled toward the aisle, I was

THE HARRY POTTER MOVIE

wrestling with the question. *Do I jump up? Should I tag along and make sure he doesn't wander off?*

Yes. No. Yes.

For him to be safe, I should have gone. But I wanted to demonstrate some trust. He didn't leave when I had gone to the restroom earlier, so why should I follow him? Finally, I decided to stay put and respect his privacy. As Mike headed off to the restroom, I tried to reassure myself that he would be okay.

Ten of the longest minutes of my life ticked by. Where was Mike? Despite all the magical preparations Hogwarts students were making to keep demons away, my own demon was tightening its grip on me when Mike didn't return.

"Very well," Dumbledore told the students. "Good luck to you all. Mr. Diggory, at the sound of the cannon, you may pro-"

KA-BLOOM!

The cannon blast in the film made me flinch. The storyline's building tension didn't compare with the one inside me, sitting alone in the darkness. *Where the hell is Mike?* I went to look for him.

The theater lobby was quiet. Two workers at the snack bar chatted lazily while waiting for customers. Mike wasn't there. My heart was pounding, and I fought down panic. The restroom was silent.

"Mike?"

No response. I checked the stalls. Every one was empty.

"Damn it!"

I scanned the lobby, then the dark theater.

Maybe he got lost, sat in the wrong row.

I struggled to calm down as I walked to the front of the theater and turned around. The crowd of faces was illuminated by flickers of bouncing light, none of them Mike. I tried the other aisle. No Mike.

What do I do now?

After another trip to the restroom and a re-check of the lobby, I rushed down the hall to the theater's video game arcade, but Mike was nowhere to be found. My trust in him, my respect for his privacy, had backfired. I had no choice but to call 9-1-1.

****

"He's about six feet tall, two hundred pounds, part-Native American . . ." My eyes scanned the crowd milling behind the cop as I went down my mental checklist. Height, weight, eye color, clothes—anything I could think of to help him find Mike.

"He's a patient at Western State."

"Oh, an *ESCAPEE*," the cop said flatly.

He glanced at me momentarily, then looked down and added that fact to the notes he was making. Whatever happened to Mike was not a priority in a shopping mall full of Christmas shoppers.

"No, he's not an escapee. He was out—" There was no way to avoid telling him. "See, I took him out on a pass."

The cop stared at me, and his look said it all: *What fool would take a mental patient to a movie and then let him wander away?* Any other time the cop's facial expression would have pissed me off, but I was too busy asking myself that question. And feeling sick with guilt.

"Here's my cell number," I said and handed him my business card. As stupid as I felt, standing there wasn't going to find Mike. "And here's the number for the ward at the hospital. Thanks for your help."

"We'll let you know if we find him," he said. He stuffed his notes into his shirt pocket and walked away.

Embarrassed and worried as I was, I didn't care what he thought. I felt horrible, felt like it was all my fault. I just wanted to find Mike, who could be anywhere. *God, please help them find Mike, and let him be okay.*

32

Footsteps Approach

6 pm, December 8, 2005

The footsteps stopped and keys rattled behind the door. Various versions of what I was going to tell them raced through my mind.

A thick fog had started rolling in as daylight evaporated, so after three fruitless hours of searching for Mike, I gave up. It was time to return to Western State and face the music.

I was worn out. Mike was missing. And I was mortified that I had lost one of Western State's patients, especially one entrusted to my care.

"Hi, I'm Dennis. Mike's Big Brother, and—"

The male staff member cut me off.

"Oh, we just got horrible news about Michael." His tone was hushed, and his words slugged me in the gut. An eerie quiet hung in the long, empty hall behind him.

"What happened?"

"Come in."

He's going to tell me Mike is dead, probably hit by a car. It's all my fault.

"We just got a call—" Suddenly he stopped talking and looked directly at me. "Did Michael sign a medical confidentiality release for you?"

"No. I don't think he did."

"Oh." End of conversation.

"What happened?" I insisted, trying to hide my panic.

135

"Let me go talk with my supervisor."

"Is he okay?"

"I'll have to check with my supervisor."

My heart pounded. This was the spot where a few hours earlier they let me take Mike out in public without any restrictions, but now was fortified with an invisible wall against me.

Two dazed patients walked past, their curiosity piqued by a nighttime visitor. The only sounds came from inside the nurses' station, where the staff spoke in hushed voices as they flipped through Mike's medical file. They could flip pages all night, but they wouldn't find it. Mike had not signed an information release.

"I'm sorry," the supervisor said when she and the male staff member returned. "We can't release any information."

"Wait a minute! You let me take him on a pass, and I've just spent all afternoon looking for him. Then I come back here and you tell me you have horrible news, and you won't tell me what happened without a release?"

"We can't release any information," she repeated.

"Is he okay?"

"Really, we can't." They paused and shared an uncomfortable glance. The supervisor was squirming.

"They are going to bring him back here later tonight," she finally said.

So, he is alive. Thank God.

"Is he okay?" I begged.

"Really, I can't say anything without a release."

"Is there anyone else I can talk to?"

She slammed the file shut, shot me a disgusted glance, and let the silence hang in the air. I knew our discussion was over.

"You can try the administrative nurse on duty," she said coldly. "Go to the reception office in the next building. I'll call to let them know you're coming."

"Thank you. I really appreciate the help."

I meant it. It wasn't the first time the lack of a release had blocked me when I needed to know what was up with Mike. But tonight it was urgent.

****

The hush inside the administrative waiting room offered a small buffer from the chaos that filled this massive old hospital. Knowing that Mike was coming back had calmed me down. It meant he was alive. That was all that mattered. *At least I hadn't killed him.*

She was certainly not the hardened Nurse Ratchet I expected to see. I introduced myself, and she nodded as I explained what happened. It gave me some hope that she would tell me about Mike. Finally, she spoke.

"I wish I could share more information," she said. "But legally we can't."

"I understand, but he was out with me when he walked off. They told me something horrible happened. I think I have the right to know what it was."

"I can tell you that Mike is coming back here later tonight. He would not be brought back if he wasn't medically able to be here. You understand that, don't you?" She was trying to help, telling me what she could.

"Yes, I understand."

"What I can do is to ask Mike to call you when he gets here."

"Thank you, I'd appreciate that. I feel responsible for what happened."

"Just be aware that all I can do is ask him if he wants to call you. He will make the decision."

****

The fog on the drive home was unrelenting, and it took my full concentration just to stay on the road. The shroud of mystery foggy nights created was often energizing, but tonight it just added a nervous edge to a horrible day.

An unpleasant bleating from my cell phone broke the silence. The caller ID flashed "Restricted Number." I pulled off the road and answered.

"Dennis?"

"Yes, this is Dennis."

"I have Michael with me here at the hospital, and he would like to talk to you. Hold on."

There was a brief pause.

"Hello." His voice had its usual flat tone.

"Mike?"

"Uh-huh."

"Hi, buddy. Thanks for calling me."
"Yeah."
"Are you all right? I was so worried about you."
"Uh-huh."
"What happened, Mike?"
"I was at Safeway, and drank some Clorox chlorine bleach."
"What?"
"I went to Safeway and I drink some Clorox chlorine bleach."
"You drank bleach?" Tears stung my eyes. *This was my fault.*
"Uh-huh."
"What happened?" I cried. "Why?"
"I was thinking everything would be past, but then it wasn't. So, I decided I would drink some bleach."
"Where, where did . . .? Did someone find you?"
"The lady sees me and took it."
"The lady? A worker in Safeway?"
"No, a . . ." He was grasping for the word.
"A shopper?"
"Yeah, one of them. She take the bleach."
"Before you drank it? Or did you already drink some?"
"After I drinked it."
"How much did you drink?"
"I drinked about a pint of Clorox chlorine bleach."
"Did you go to the hospital?"
"Uh-huh."
"What did they say?"
"They take me back here."
"I'm so sorry that happened, buddy. Are you okay right now?"
"I am okay."
"Mike, why did you drink bleach?"
"I was thinking everything of the past would be good. But then it wasn't. So, I decided, I decide I drink bleach."
"Were you trying to hurt yourself, Mike?" A stupid question, but I wasn't

thinking straight.

"Yeah. I decided I would kill myself. So I drink some Clorox chlorine bleach."

"I'm glad you are back at the hospital, Mike. You get some rest. I'll talk to you in a couple days."

"Okay."

"I love you, Mike." It was the only thing I could say.

Click. The other side of the line went dead, and I started sobbing as my emotions smacked me. Swirling waves of guilt, shame, anger collided with the relief I felt that Mike was somehow still alive. It took me a while to wipe my tears, try to collect myself, and resume the drive home. *At least Mike was alive.*

I was horrified, stunned and in shock. I felt stupid for even thinking it was a good idea to take Mike—a mental patient—out of Western State. But never in my wildest imagination did I even think it was possible that the day would have ended like this.

33

Sounding the Alarm

Just as his fingers touched the black queen, an electronic buzzer started bleating. Behind the locked steel door separating Mike and me from the television room, the fire alarm was going off.

With every flash of the strobe light above the door behind Mike, my last bits of denial flickered away. There was no sign the buzzing would let up soon, and on the other side of the door voices were escalating with excitement.

"Is that the fire alarm, Mike?"

"Yeah." He didn't seem concerned.

Mike's gaze shifted slowly to the flashing light over the door behind him. Then he stared back at me.

"What are you supposed to do when this happens, Mike?"

"Go to the room."

"Which room?"

"That one." Mike pointed over his shoulder.

"Where the TV is?"

"Yeah."

Two windows in our visitor's room looked out into the hallway. Residents and staff members scurried about, but it was impossible to tell which way they were going.

"How about we call this game a tie and pack it up, Mike?"

We swept the pieces off the wooden chessboard into a plastic bag. Mike's

SOUNDING THE ALARM

glare intensified with every honk of the fire alarm. I wondered what was going through his mind. When I stood up, he looked startled.

"What about the money?" he asked. There was a hint of panic in his voice.

"Oh, I almost forgot. I pulled out my wallet and handed Mike a $20 bill. A slight smile momentarily crossed his face. Then he peered nervously at the windows, made sure no one was watching, bent over, and hid the bill in his sock.

"Thanks."

"You're welcome, Mike."

HYPOCRITE. *It's HIS money.*

Mike did not know that for the past few months, I had been the payee for his Social Security benefits. He didn't even know he received the benefits. He had no clue that now he was the one paying for any items he asked for. Whenever he thanked me, I had to reassure myself that it was okay. While he was locked up here with his care covered, there was no reason for him to know about the money. My role was to make sure he got everything he needed, and the remainder went into his account.

A madhouse greeted us as soon as we opened the door.

"It's just a drill," a staff guy whispered. "Go ahead and stay in there."

We returned to our usual places on opposite sides of the table. Mike immediately began setting up the chess pieces. The buzzing continued non-stop.

"That noise is annoying, isn't it?"

"Yeah," Mike mumbled without looking up. "The first one at night was an hour and a half."

"Here, on this floor? An hour and a half?"

"Uh-huh."

"Did they make you go outside?"

"No."

"Was it a drill?"

"Yeah. We stayed in the room."

He was still a man of few words but had been more conversant lately. He called me three times the previous week asking for video game strategy books, the only things he read. He said he liked learning game moves. I believed what enthralled him was the invincibility of the characters, their powers, and their magical fantasy lives. He lived vicariously through them.

There were other changes in Mike during the last few weeks. He started watching TV news, and for the first time in his eleven months at Western State he wasn't resting in his room all day.

I was concerned by the changes. In the past, as Mike's verbal communication increased, so did his unpredictable behavior. Once his medications tapered down, he started breaking out of his shell, but before long, his path started taking very weird turns.

"You notice he's improving," his caseworker told me over the phone last week. *No way. He's still a mess.*

"I noticed he seemed more talkative."

It scared me that the medical staff felt he was doing better. Maybe under their constant watch they were seeing progress I couldn't, but what happened if he "improved" to the point they let him go? Where would he end up?

Mike's evolving mental state was like our chess matches. The pieces were always the same, the moves rarely differed. But the strategy was constantly shifting. Mike made his moves. The game changed and I would react. And I was left asking myself, "What do I do? Is there even anything I can do?"

****

I tried to focus on our game, but the alarm continued to blare and the staff tried to contain the panic. A karaoke machine came to life, and someone hollered, "Let's sing a song we all know!"

Rudolph, the red-nose reindeer,

Had a very shiny nose.

And if you ever saw it,

You would even say it glows!

Mike captured my knight. He was on a roll. It was my turn to move, but my options weren't looking good. I sensed Mike had a trick up his sleeve, he always did. I moved my bishop, but it was a mistake.

All of the other reindeer

Used to laugh and call him names.

SOUNDING THE ALARM

They wouldn't let poor Rudolph
Join in any reindeer games.
"Check."

I slid my king behind a pawn. The singing continued, and there were no good options.

Then one foggy Christmas Eve
Santa came to say,
Rudolph with your . . .

HEY!" a patient screamed. "WHY ARE WE SINGING THIS SONG? IT'S NOT CHRISTMAS!"

No kidding! It's September 4 and it's eighty degrees outside. I am sitting locked in the state mental hospital with the fire alarm going off. For the umpteenth time in the past two and a half years, I am getting my butt whipped in chess. By a guy who won't take a bath and wants to become an arcade game character. A choir of panicked psychiatric patients is serenading us with "Rudolph the Red Nosed Reindeer." Just who the hell is the crazy one here?

Mike moved his queen one space. "That's checkmate."

"You're the champ, Mike!" I shook his hand.

"I am, aren't I?"

As much as it frustrated me to lose, I admired his ability. It helped to see Mike smile, to know that for a moment, his day was spiced with a flicker of triumph.

Fifteen minutes later, the fire alarm finally stopped during the first verse of *"White Christmas."* Mike's queen zipped diagonally across the board, and they finally turned the karaoke machine off.

"That's checkmate, isn't it?"

I mentally moved every piece I had left. Yes, it was checkmate—again. Mike notched up his third win of this visit.

"Good job. Shall we call it a day?"

"Yeah. A day."

"I enjoyed our time today, Mike. Thanks."

"Me too."

We tossed the pieces into the plastic bag and slid it into the cardboard box with the chessboard.

****

We stepped out of our locked room to find that calm had been restored to the ward. Four dazed residents sat with their gazes locked on the large TV screen. I scanned the hall for a staff member to unlock the ward door and call the elevator.

Mike stood under the glaring fluorescent hallway light, in his dirty gold sweatshirt, his favorite green sweatpants, and well-worn black tennis shoes with Velcro straps unfastened.

For some reason, I didn't feel an urge to rush off like I often did. We shared a hug and the special Big Brother handshake that had ended every get-together since the day we met thirteen years ago.

"I'll see you in two weeks," I promised.

"Uh . . ." Mike hesitated. Something was going through his mind. What was it? Maybe he was going to tell me not to come back.

"Yeah," he finally muttered. "Yeah. Two weeks."

"Okay, buddy. Take care of yourself."

"I will."

As the elevator door opened, I looked back to see Mike shuffling off toward his room. The box containing his little wooden chessboard was tucked safely under his arm.

"Did you have a nice visit?" the staff member asked me.

"Yes, it was good, except for the fire drill. Thank you, and thanks for your help with Mike."

"You're welcome," she said with a smile. A quick twist of her key and the elevator whirred to life, moving down to set me free.

The elevator rides were always the same, only my feelings changed. Sometimes I started crying before I reached my truck. Other days the sadness was there but tears would not flow. Usually I was just numb, in a hurry to start my truck and drive off to anyplace but Western State.

This time, for some reason I felt content. Mike and I had a good time together, all things considered. He seemed to be doing fairly well, but his hesitation when I told him I'd see him in two weeks bothered me. It felt odd.

I enjoyed my visit. It was a relief to see him, and I knew that as long as Mike was locked inside of the hospital he was safe.

I couldn't ask for anything more than that.

34

September 6, 2006

Right in the middle of adding finishing touches to a marketing piece I was writing, the phone rang.

"Is this Dennis?"

"Yes, it's Dennis. Who is this?"

"This is ah-Sally, ah-case-worker for ah-Michael."

Her thick Asian accent and broken English made her hard to understand. It took a few seconds to realize she was a caseworker from Western State Hospital.

"I'm calling tell you Michael walked away from hospital grounds today, so is on status of unauthorized leave. I already call Mrs. Scott and tell her."

"What do you mean? He left? What happened?"

"He walk away during free time. So, he is now unauthorized leave."

"When did he leave?"

"Today. This morning."

I could visualize the scene in my mind. *Mike was outside on this hot, sunny day dressed in his sweats and tennis shoes. He was wandering the courtyard with a couple other patients. He carefully watched the staff member who was supervising the few patients who had earned the right to go out for a few minutes of fresh air. He waited for the right moment, when the staff would be distracted. When they weren't watching, he slipped between the old red brick buildings, then bolted across four lanes of traffic on Steilacoom Boulevard to freedom.*

"Okay, thanks for letting me know. Please call me if you hear anything from him."

"Yes, we will. Bye now."

I felt so helpless. The hospital's job was to notify Betty, so technically their call to me was a courtesy. I knew Mike was not the first one to walk away from Western State, and he wouldn't be the last. He knew as well as I did that Western State didn't have a posse to go round up missing patients. As soon as Mike disappeared, he was free, could roam the streets at will until he had a chance encounter with the cops or decided on his own to come back.

Damn! Why the hell did he run off? Then again, why wouldn't he?

I knew why. He was sick and tired of being locked up twenty-four hours a day with people telling him what to do and not to do. *Who could blame him?*

It ticked me off because it was a hassle I didn't need right then. I was getting ready to leave town the next day with Joe. We were going on a long-planned pilgrimage to Norman, Oklahoma, for a Washington Husky football game. But Mike didn't care.

A conversation I had with him a few years earlier popped into my mind. "Mike, the next time you run away, I'm not coming looking. I'm not playing hide and seek. You can call me to let me know you are okay or if you want to meet. But I'm done running around looking for you, understand?"

"Yeah, okay." He nodded.

I meant it. After the call from the hospital case worker, I tried to put runaway Mike out of my mind. If he didn't show up by the time Joe and I got back from Oklahoma, then I'd see what I could do, but I wasn't about to let him ruin our trip.

I thought about Betty. Should I call her? It would be a nice gesture, but probably pointless. The hospital had already notified her, and there was nothing either one of us could do. Given her recent memory problems, I didn't know what she would comprehend. I gave up and went back to my work.

****

Half an hour later the phone rang. *Maybe it's him.* That was my reaction every time Mike went missing.

"Dennis? It's Betty." Her voice was weak.

Damn, why didn't I call her first?

"Hi, Betty."

"Mike walked away from the hospital and is still missing."

"Yeah. The hospital called me too. They said they had already talked to you."

"You haven't heard from him, have you?"

"No. They said he walked away during his time outside today, and I really don't know where he would go. He could be just about anywhere."

"I don't know why they let him go outside by himself."

"They usually go out in a group with the staff, Betty. He probably just took off from the group."

"No. I thought they said he was out by himself."

Her memory was failing, and facts tended to get scrambled.

"No, I'm sure he was with a group. There's no way they would ever let him outside on his own."

"Oh. Okay."

"Betty, Joe and I are leaving town tomorrow for a football game in Oklahoma. I'm not going to be around for a few days, but I'll check my messages when I'm gone. If I hear anything, I'll let you know right away."

"That sounds good."

"I'm sure he'll show up eventually. Try not to worry too much. He'll show up."

"I hope so."

"It's always one adventure after the next with him, isn't it?"

"It sure is," she laughed. "Are you going to visit your family in Montana?"

"No. We're going to Oklahoma for a football game."

"Oh, that sounds fun."

"I'll be in touch. You take care and don't worry, okay?"

"All right. Thanks, guy. I love you."

"I love you too."

35

A Newspaper Sketch

September 13, 2006

She was crying on the other end of the line. Between her sobs, I could make out what she was saying, but I didn't want to believe it.

"There was a sketch. In the paper this morning. They're trying to identify a guy who jumped off the Aurora Avenue Bridge." Linda's voice trembled. "It, it was him. It was Mike. He's dead."

"Are you sure?" I was stunned.

"I am. I was reading the paper and saw the sketch. It's him."

I couldn't talk.

"I called the number," she continued, "and told them it was him. Two other people had already called and said it was him, a teacher and a past caseworker. There's no mistake. It is Mike."

"Does Betty know yet?"

"She knows. She's a bit confused, but she understands. She is crushed."

"Joe and I will come up to be with you. I just can't believe it. When did it happen?"

"The day he ran away from Western State. Somehow he made it up to Seattle. Then he jumped off the bridge."

My head was spinning, the morning dissolved into a blur. Joe walked in as I hung up. He didn't even need to ask. I was sobbing.

"It was Linda. There was a sketch in the paper of Mike. He jumped off the

Aurora Bridge last week. He's dead."

We shared a hug, took a few deep breaths, and Joe started to cry with me. He knew how much Mike meant to me, how much he meant to both of us.

We pulled ourselves together and headed off to Seattle to try to comfort Betty and Linda. Along the way we bought a copy of the morning *Seattle Post-Intelligencer* and flipped through the pages. Our hopes that it was a mistake were shattered by a blurb in the "Northwest Briefs." "Public's Help Sought to ID Suicide Victim." The artist's sketch attached was definitely Mike. His face appeared relaxed, and he was smiling.

****

I first walked into Betty's home in 1992 full of hope and excitement. I was eager to take Mike places, to teach him to throw a football, to water-ski, to help him learn to ride a bike. If all went well, I was even going to do God's work by helping him learn to love the University of Washington Huskies.

Now, nearly fourteen years later, I walked into her home on a September afternoon crippled with grief. The unthinkable end that I so often feared had finally happened. I stepped into Betty's home a wiser man whose life had been changed forever by her adopted son.

Joe and I sat with Betty for hours, trying to console her and ourselves by telling stories of times with Mike. Jake the Poodle stayed with us, poking us for pats like he always did. He could sense our grief and was trying to help.

Two days later Linda, her brother Tom and I went to the funeral home where Mike's body had been transferred. As soon as we sat down, the funeral director informed us they had already received Mike's body. That news triggered a struggle inside me, fighting the urge to see his body, just to be sure it wasn't a mistake. My denial was raging; my common sense finally convinced me not to do it.

Linda and Tom arranged for Mike's cremation and settled a few other details. Their family made plans for me to have a small amount of his ashes. They are still in my home today, in a mahogany urn with a photo on the front of Mike holding Jake.

After the meeting, I went to Pike Place market, bought a bouquet of flowers, and placed them under the Aurora Avenue bridge in honor of Mike. Then

A NEWSPAPER SKETCH

I sat down in the morning sun and sobbed. I had tried my best, but was devastated. My Big Brother match had finally come to this.

36

The Chessboard

Four days after learning Mike was dead, I went to Western State to pick up his few possessions. As I drove into the hospital complex, a flood of relief hit me because Mike was no longer one of the dazed people suffering inside. Even deep in my grief, I understood that he was finally free. His spirit would not have to spend another day locked up in these depressing buildings.

Walking into the ward, I noticed the staff members were in a hushed mood, trying to avoid eye contact. I felt for them, understanding that the death of a patient they had all worked with must have been an enormous shock. Another fact may have intensified their feelings. Just as Betty had told me the day he'd gone missing, Mike had indeed been allowed outside alone for free time when he escaped from Western State. He was allowed to go outside unsupervised for the first time after two and a half years of being kept inside locked wards. Mike just walked away, made his way to Seattle, and killed himself. I believed I knew how guilty they must feel.

Two cardboard boxes. The entire physical effects of Mike's life were crammed into just two cardboard boxes. The larger one held his clothing, the smaller one his possessions. I was sobbing uncontrollably when I left. Tears still flowed when I pulled into my driveway. I have no idea how I drove home.

Before the unopened boxes went into my garage to be kept out of sight,

THE CHESSBOARD

there was one item I wanted. The chessboard. The hours we spent on either side of that little wooden board anchored our friendship all those years behind locked doors.

Reaching deep into the cardboard box, I found the smaller one that held the precious chessboard. The pieces were still wrapped where Mike and I put them less than two weeks ago. The king, the queen, the pawns, all snuggled together in a plastic bag waiting for the next time Mike and I would match wits at the chessboard. Mike had the board tucked under his arm as he shuffled down the hospital hall away from me the last time I ever saw him.

I started sifting through the box. All Mike's worldly possessions were inside, pieces of his illness. One shower slipper, five broken crayons, a few scattered chess pieces from a previous set. Among the loose papers that fluttered among the mess, one official-looking form caught my attention. It was a signed copy from his most recent legal hearings on his confinement at Western State, agreeing to extend his commitment. It was folded and crumpled from being carried for days inside his pocket.

That paper shocked me. I imagined just how alone Mike must have felt, having to go through that hearing by himself. I fell to my knees and sobbed. *I tried so hard to make him feel loved, to know that he had a friend. How much difference did I make?*

****

By the end of his life, Mike was disconnected from the world and the people surrounding him, even me. He didn't seem to understand or even care about the consequences of his actions.

"Look at how many people's lives were touched by knowing him or coming in contact with him during the time we knew Mike," Joe said to me shortly after Mike died, trying his best to comfort me.

"Even my Little Brother Nate. I remember the first time they got together and Mike locked Nate with the dogs inside their kennel," Joe reminisced. "Nate was so mad that he was screaming and started insulting Mike about his speech. Yet as time went on, being with Mike really helped Nate. Not only did he become more compassionate, Nate often went out of his way to help Mike. He worked hard to help Mike feel comfortable when they were together. It made me feel better to know there are so many people Mike brought together. I think that was the glory of being Michael."

****

Mike did, in ways, have a Lucky Life. The state foster system brought him to Betty, and she saved him by taking him into her heart and home. From that point forward, Mike felt an enormous amount of love and caring from a diverse group of family and friends, including me. That support—all of it—was given freely from people who were not Mike's blood relatives.

The time I spent with Mike was one of the great gifts of my life. I miss him more than I ever dreamed I would. I often recall playing chess in the bizarre confines of the psychiatric hospitals. I envision his happy flapping arms as a child. Gone forever is the cozy warmth of sitting together on Betty's couch drawing stick figures to record our outings. I miss all the negotiation it would take to end his stalling to keep me from leaving when our outings ended. How he told me he loved me.

In my bedroom Mike's chessboard is set up on my dresser, in a place of honor among my treasured pictures, a small lamp, and the occasional loose change, pen, or wallet. That chessboard keeps him in my daily life.

The pieces are set up for the next game, the white ones facing out into my room. A single black pawn near the queen is positioned one space forward. That was the move Mike used to launch our games at Western State. Whenever the pieces get jolted askew on the board, I reset them exactly to that position. They are a tribute to Mike, reminding me to make a start, move forward, and carry on.

37

Bringing Mike Home

Wham! Every bump on the freeway caused a different emotion. I couldn't decide if I wanted to laugh or cry, and had already done plenty of both. My mind and my feelings drifted at will, returning suddenly to the hospital I visited two hours ago.

"You know about Mike don't you?"

"Yes Betty," I said. I reached over and took her frail hand. "Yes, I know. I really miss him."

"I do too."

Betty looked so fragile. She stared right at me, but her gaze was somewhere far, far away. Her hospital gown was wrinkled, wisps of her long gray hair trailed off in every direction. She looked so very lost.

It had been a month since Mike died, and she occasionally forgot that Joe and I knew. Her memories of distant yesterdays remained intact, but every passing day scrambled recent events a bit more. My hope was that her failing memory helped ease the pain of missing Mike.

Holding her hand gave me strength as I shared her grief. She was a real angel. She had saved Mike's life by welcoming him into her home as a two-year-old foster child, and gave him a chance to thrive there. It hurt to see her suffer.

THUNK! The truck hit a pothole and shifted the box in the back seat. *Be careful, Dennis!* I didn't have to remind myself that I couldn't let anything happen to my precious cargo.

I was finally bringing Mike home. After all his shuffling between group homes, foster care and psychiatric hospitals, Mike would have a home with Joe and me. He would rest in a place where he was safe, loved, and where we'd shared some great times. It was an honor to have some of his ashes and be able to give them a resting place.

He's dead, you hypocrite! You should have at least tried to have him live with you!

My conscience kept pestering me, asking why I didn't try sooner. Nonstop thoughts of what-if scenarios. None of them had a happy ending, I knew. But that didn't help me now. *I could have done more.*

A speeding Honda made a sudden lane change, cutting off my inner monologue and my truck. *Focus on the road, Dennis!* The squealing brakes reminded me I wasn't in the driver's seat on Mike's life journey. Wrecks happened. I could not control his mental illness, and I could not have prevented his death. I did the best I could for him.

What I did do for him was the only thing I could. I showed up. Week after week, for over thirteen years, I shared some time with him. What more could I have done?

We had shared a spiritual journey. Of all the drives he and I took together over the years, this was one of the most therapeutic. Mike's struggles were finally over. I was bringing him home, giving him a place where his gentle spirit could be free to roam as it chose. I started to feel calm.

****

Excited whines from the dog kennel welcomed me home. Our shelter dogs Lucy, (a brown, splotchy colored, laid-back Catahoula mix), and Bonz, (an escape-and-run artist disguised as a yellow lab mix) would have to remain in the kennel for now. I brought the cardboard box inside and set it on the kitchen counter.

Outside the open kitchen window, gentle waves lapped on the shore of Henderson Bay. The view was an ever-changing scene of blue and green accented with sprinkles of autumn gold. The soothing sound of water massaging the beach broke the silence.

Like a kid cautiously opening a birthday gift, I slowly pulled out the packing paper. Halfway into the box, I found a folder from the funeral home, decorated with warm brown colors and adorned with a small black lantern on the cover. I set it aside and kept digging.

"There!"

My probing fingers touched the little urn. I pulled it out and peeled away the thin protective wrapping. I set the shiny mahogany-colored urn on the counter, took a step back, and said,

"Welcome home Mike . . ."

I sobbed. All that remained of my buddy Mike was in that urn. Emotion overwhelmed me, and I wished this was not happening. Why? Why did it have to end like this?

It was hard to dial the numbers with my trembling hand. The urn on the counter filled me with horror. I wanted to crawl into a hole and sleep forever. I needed to talk to Joe.

"This is Joe."

"Joe?" I said weakly. "What you doing?"

"Just working. You?"

"I, I just brought Mike home .. ." I broke down crying again.

"Oh." The spirit evaporated from his voice. "You all right, buddy?"

"Yeah," I sobbed. "It just feels so . . . so sad."

"I know." Joe was obviously trying not to cry.

"I just needed to call. I needed to hear your voice."

"I'm glad you did. Do you want me to come home?"

"No. That's okay. I'm going to lie down for a while."

"I think that's a good idea."

"I'll be okay, really. I just needed to hear your voice. I love you."

"I love you, Dennis." Just what I needed to know.

****

The funeral home folder caught my eye again when I hung up.

NO! Wait until later! But I had to look inside.

It was just an ordinary folder, with subtle colors blended together in a careful, sympathetic pattern. Not too depressing, not too cheerful, perfect for a company that made its money as a rest stop for corpses.

WAIT Dennis! This isn't a good time . . .

The cover letter inside was three paragraphs, written in flowery words chosen to gently mute its simple message:

We are so very sorry. If anyone else you know drops dead, please give us a call.

Three certified copies of Mike's death certificate were behind the letter. Except for their color, they looked exactly like the title to a used car.

THERE! Tucked behind the death certificates I spied my Holy Grail. I grabbed it, afraid to open it. I was holding a copy of the Seattle Police Department's report on Mike's death.

38

The Police Report

The only clues to the mystery of September 6 were on that paper. Nervously I opened the official record of the last afternoon of Mike's life.

The report staring back at me looked eerily empty; many of the information blocks were blank. Like so much of Mike's life, too many pieces of the puzzle were missing.

- Time occurred: 4:01 pm, Wednesday, September 6, 2006.
- Time reported: 4:02 pm, Wednesday, September 6, 2006.
- Victim's name: John Doe, White, and Male, in his 30's.

Details in a few boxes were blacked out, obscuring the identity of a lone witness who was the last person to see Mike alive.

The officer's description made me sick to my stomach:

I was dispatched to the report of a person who had jumped off the Aurora Bridge. Victim Doe landed in the westbound lanes of travel on Westlake Ave. North in the 2700 block. Doe was wearing a maroon sweat suit with black tennis shoes. Witness observed Doe falling at approximately 50-feet off the ground before impact as he drove eastbound on Westlake Ave. North.

King County Medical Examiner's office was called . . . Investigator Midkiff did search Doe for any form of identification finding none. Only a bus pass and club card with no name or other identifying information was located on the victim . . . Midkiff removed Doe's body to the Medical Examiner's office.

A few signatures and a case number on the bottom made the whole thing official. Another notation jumped off the page at me:

"2 rolls of 35mm film at the scene, which have been submitted to the Police Department photo lab for processing."

I should get those pictures. I should see if it was really him.

I struggled to clear that notion from my mind. Standing alone in my kitchen, I was besieged by visions of the horrid scene; I didn't need to see it on film.

****

When I turned to the second page of the report, my heart skipped. There was a sketch, a full-page drawing. A diagonal line bisecting the page was noted as the Aurora Bridge. Lines dividing east- and westbound traffic ran from the bridge to the top of the paper. Another line showed the edge of the two westbound lanes, with dashes added to illustrate lane dividers. The twelve-foot width of the lane was carefully noted, as was the location of a light pole off to the right. My eyes froze on a spot where something was added to the drawing just above the diagonal line.

It was the last moment in the life of my precious Little Brother. The end of Mike's life was forever recorded on the police department sketch staring right at me.

Lying spread-eagle on the westbound lanes was a stick figure. His head was resting on the centerline.

A stick figure.

It was Mike.

V

Time Moves On

*It is both a blessing and a curse
to feel everything so deeply.*

39

Betty's Passing

The phone rang just as I was stepping into the shower. On the fourth ring, the answering machine kicked on, and I paused to listen as it recorded the call.

"Hi guy, it's Linda. I just wanted to give you a heads up that mom is in her last days. Hospice was here yesterday, and Tommy is flying in from New York today. I wanted to let you know in case you want to come say goodbye in the next day or two. But I wouldn't wait too long."

"Did you hear that?" Joe hollered from upstairs. There was panic in his voice.

"Yeah, I heard it."

It was five minutes after nine on Groundhog's Day, a lazy Saturday morning. I had not even taken a shower yet, and the Groundhog must have popped up. Apparently he had seen his shadow and decided it was time for many more months of mourning.

I started crying in the shower as sadness washed over me. Betty was dying. She was my last tie to Mike.

It was not a surprise. Each time I visited her in the past two years, her decline was more pronounced. She had been slipping, both mentally and physically.

"I don't think Betty will be around much longer," Joe said during our drive home after a December visit. Yet the call from Linda that morning was a shock.

This couldn't be possible. Linda had to be exaggerating.

It took tremendous concentration for me to finish showering. My mind was fragmented into confused thoughts. I wanted to stay in the shower forever and avoid having to return Linda's call.

****

"Uh, hi, Linda. I got your message."

"Yeah. I wanted to let you know it's getting close."

"How is she now? Is she conscious?"

"She's doing okay. She was sitting up and talking earlier but is sleeping now. We had hospice in and got a hospital bed set up."

"What did the hospice people say?"

"They've been great, they came in and got everything set up. They let us know what to expect about the dying process. They seemed to think it will be in the next day or so."

"How about if I come up this afternoon? Would that work?"

"Sure, hon. Come anytime."

Her voice sounded solid. There was none of the quivering I heard when she called after seeing the sketch of Mike in the newspaper eighteen months ago.

Joe hugged me after I hung up.

"I am so sorry, buddy. So very, very sorry."

****

Four hours later, Joe and I walked up the steps of the North Seattle home Betty shared with Linda and her husband Chris. The sun was shining, but an unrelenting gloom hung in the air. We shared hugs with Linda, Chris, and Betty's son David. They led us into the open family room where Betty lay on the hospital bed. Soft music played as she slept, breathing rhythmically.

Joe and I sat down beside her. We held her hand and told her we loved her. She continued sleeping. As we sat at her bedside, Betty's six-year-old great grandson Damien sauntered into the room and moved up to her bed.

"How are you Damien?" I asked.

"Good!" he said.

BETTY'S PASSING

Damien looked at Betty, then at the small table next to her bed. He pointed to a small sponge on a stick which was used to moisten Betty's lips.

"See that thing?" he asked. "Well, there is an extra one. And if Great Grandma dies today, I get to have it!"

"Oh?"

I could tell Joe was trying not to laugh. If Betty was conscious, she would have rolled her eyes. We knew she too would have thought it was hilarious that the kid's only thought was that he was going to score the extra sponge if she kicked the bucket.

The afternoon vigil passed slowly in a blur of quiet conversations, soft music, and time next to Betty, holding her hand.

Around 4:30, Linda took a phone call.

"That was my brother Tom. They're in Seattle and on their way."

"Joe and I are heading out for a while. We want you and your brothers to have some time with your mom. We'll be back later."

****

After two hours of driving aimlessly around Seattle, we went back to Betty's. Words were hard to come by, our thoughts scattered. Joe and I decided we would check in with the family, visit for a short time, then go home.

Betty's condition was unchanged. She had not regained consciousness since that morning. The revolving change of guard at her bedside continued. When Tom and his partner arrived, all her family were there.

"My Favorite Things" from *The Sound of Music* floated from the stereo. Joe and I had been back at the house for half an hour. As I sat next to her and watched her breathing, it seemed to be slowing.

"Hey, Joe, tell Linda to come here. I think she's dying!"

The family gathered around Betty's bed, and Linda and her brothers held her hands. Betty slowly stopped breathing, and then she was gone.

It was so peaceful. It was as if she had waited to pass until Tom arrived so they could all be together.

Her journey had come to an end. We all gathered in the kitchen a few feet from where her body lay on the bed. We shared hugs, tears, and memories.

As we grieved together, no one noticed Damien. He stood at Betty's bedside for a few seconds staring at her motionless body, then he climbed up next to her.

Like a trampoline artist, Damien started jumping up and down on the mattress.

"Yep, SHE'S DEAD!" he hollered, shattering the silence. "SHE'S DEAD ALL RIGHT. SHE'S REALLY DEAD!"

"DAMIEN!" Linda screamed. "Get off NOW!"

"SHE'S DEAD! I WANT TO MAKE SURE SHE'S DEAD!"

Linda bolted across the room ready to kill him, but tears in the kitchen changed into laughter. It was just too funny!

Somewhere beyond that kitchen filled with laughter, Betty was smiling. The family that made her life so special was celebrating her memory with the same love and laughter she shared so often with every one of us. A fitting tribute indeed.

40

Bidding Goodbye

Three weeks after her passing, Betty's children, Linda, David, and Tom, hosted a Celebration of Life event. It was a crisp, sunny February day, the venue a restaurant on the water at Seattle's Shilshole Bay. The majestic Olympic Mountain range was the backdrop for serene views of passing boats on Puget Sound. Betty would have loved it.

Three generations of Betty's family were there to honor her, including great-grandson Damien, on his best behavior. A large gathering of her friends and family members attended, a great tribute to Betty. Joe and I were honored to be included, grateful for the wonderful woman who had touched our lives so deeply.

After the tributes and meal, we joined Linda and her brothers in scattering the ashes of Betty, Mike, and Jake the Poodle together in Puget Sound. Joe and I were deeply touched that Linda asked Joe and me to pour Mike's ashes. A small whirlpool suddenly formed, stirring the water, and mixing Mike's ashes with Betty's and Jake's. It was a fitting send-off for the three of them, a unique team who had bonded together to help one another in a magnificent adventure. May they be able to share each other's love and comfort forever.

41

Epilogue

What was the purpose of Mike's life? What possible reason was there for a child to arrive in this world with such great physical challenges? To be born to a mother who did not have the mental capability to care for him and a father who was long gone before Mike arrived? A kid who then had his young life marred with abuse and emotional chaos before developing serious mental illness during puberty?

The answers to those questions are above my pay grade. What I do know is I was blessed for the time I shared with Mike. It took me on a fabulous journey into a world that was vastly different from my own.

My match with Mike opened a door for me that let me observe his family's efforts to help him. Betty worked nonstop to teach Mike, find programs for him, and arrange for proper medical treatments. Along with her family, she faced life-altering decisions that had to be made for Mike's well-being, her safety, and the safety of the family.

Mike's physical journey ended on a September afternoon one hundred sixty feet below where he jumped from Seattle's Aurora Avenue Bridge. That day, Mike became a stick figure, a John Doe dead on the street. To those who didn't know him, that anonymous stick figure adequately portrayed Mike. A jumper, another suicide, another nameless guy who—for whatever reason—decided to end it all.

EPILOGUE

My purpose in writing this story was to lift that stick figure off Westlake Avenue. It was my chance to be with Mike one more time and share with others some of the magic and mystery of our journey. From the time he was young, I tried to give him a carefree safe space to enjoy himself. My role was to be a friend he could trust, someone he could count on no matter what.

The strength of a program like Big Brothers Big Sisters is the individual match between an adult and child. Those types of relationships can have a big effect on a kid's self-confidence, can help them in school, and help them develop socially. The gift to the volunteer is a clearer awareness of what is happening in the world around them. The payoff that comes with helping another navigate through the challenges of daily life is enormous.

Joe and I are blessed with the continuing friendship of our Little Brothers. We remain close friends with my first Little Brother, Scott, and his family in Minnesota, a relationship that has been ongoing since Scott and I were matched in 1980. Nate and his wife live in the Puget Sound area, which allows us to share time together frequently. Joe took seven-year-old Nate to his first Washington Husky football game in 1993. Since then, Nate, Joe, and I have traveled with the Dawgs to two Rose Bowls, road games in Michigan and California, and thirty years of home games. Nate wanted "a ten-year-old" as his Big Brother in 1992, and he got Joe. Today Nate is the same age Joe was when they were matched. The simple times Joe spent with young Nate are the foundation of the great thirty-year friendship they continue to share.

My hope is that this book will encourage readers to step forward and volunteer their time and service to help others. The time you spend can add unique payoffs to your life. No matter what that service looks like, there is always someone in every community who can use some help. My thanks go out to the staff at Big Brothers of King County who made my match with Mike possible, and to every Big Brother or Big Sister anywhere who has stepped forward to help a kid.

As Mike's illness progressed later in the match, I wrestled repeatedly with whether I was wasting my time by continuing to show up and spend time with him. Reflecting back, I know it was time well spent. The commitment to become Mike's Big Brother evolved into a successful thirteen-year lesson in acceptance. Along the way, Mike's "Big Guy in the Sky with Magical Powers"—holding his plunger and calculator—helped teach both of us a thing or two.

Along our journey I met many of the angels who work in group homes and institutions caring for the Mikes of the world. They are heroes, women and men offering comfort and care to people who others are unable to help. They toil every day in an arena where hope is hard to come by. Their work ensures that people like Mike have a safe place to stay.

To all the Eddies, Tinas, Maxes, other patients and family members that Mike and I encountered in his struggles with mental illness, my prayers go out to you. May you find hope, and may your journey be blessed with gratitude.

****

This book is dedicated to Betty. Because of her, a struggling little kid was given a unique gift. She saved his life by welcoming him into her home, sharing her love, and giving him a chance.

From the day I met her, Betty offered her unwavering support in my efforts as Mike's Big Brother. I am eternally grateful for the love and support both Joe and I received from Betty and her entire family.

Mike and I trudged along a great road together. I set out with a chubby, clean-cut little kid flapping his arms in excitement. By our final stop I was traveling with a smelly, un-bathed man wearing dirty clothes and unfastened shoes. I still could not have asked for a better companion on our journey.

I am a better man today because of Michael Scott. My prayer for Mike is that he is finally at peace.

Acknowledgments

In 1972, I mailed a fake fundraising letter to my mother that appeared to come from Richard Nixon's re-election campaign. A lifelong Democrat, she came unglued reading my carefully worded lines thanking her for being a "loyal supporter of the President" and that Nixon knew he could "count on her for a generous contribution."

The thrill of seeing her over-reaction to that letter sparked a passion. I discovered the joy of mixing words and emotions to deliver a message. It launched my writing career.

Stick Figures: A Big Brother Remembers is a touchstone along my writing journey. I would not have reached this point without the help, support, and encouragement of so many great people.

At the top of my Appreciation Roll Call is Lisa Veitenhans, my unofficial Persistence Coach. A former coworker, Lisa continually pestered me over many years with blunt questions on the progress of the book. Her unsolicited prodding was a key to finishing the work.

Many kudos to my early readers who volunteered time to read and offer suggestions on the initial draft. The feedback offered by Julie Bruey, Meagan Key, Tricia Matteson, Douglas Pope, Mazie Quinn, and Patrick Quinn was critical in smoothing out bumps in the manuscript.

I owe a debt of gratitude to Dr. Diana Marre, a fantastic mentor who provided inspiration from the start of the project. *Stick Figures: A Big Brother Remembers* began during a writing class she taught shortly after Mike died. She provided guidance and encouragement along the way, and her editing work helped complete the book.

My thanks to Michael McConnell and his professional work in the final editing and proofing of the final manuscript.

The foundation for this work was built upon the love, care and time that my parents, Jim and Dorothy Quinn, shared so freely with my siblings and me every day of our lives. The nine of us were blessed by their presence, and my folks sacrificed so much for every member of our family. Their example guided me during my times with both Scott and Mike, and in the writing of this book. The support they have given me during my life has been unwavering, and I am forever grateful to them.

Heartfelt appreciation goes out to Joe and Nate, two guys who were with Mike and me from the beginning. The memories the four of us made together still brighten our conversations when Nate, Joe, and I get together. Mike remains very much a part of our friendship, over thirty years after Big Brothers of King County brought us all together.

Words cannot express my thanks to my husband, Joe, for his years of unwavering support. He lived this story with me as it happened; he was my rock of support during Mike's illness and death. This book would not have been possible without his unconditional love, encouragement, and guidance. Joe shared generous amounts of his time and love with Mike over the years, and he played a huge part in helping Mike enjoy his Lucky Life.

About the Author

DJ Quinn is a two-time Big Brother Big Sisters volunteer, and currently assists with mentor programs in the Pierce County Juvenile Court system. Quinn's honest and humorous writing style was developed in previous editing and writing jobs for airline labor unions, lifestyle magazines, and real estate advertising. The second oldest of nine children raised in Helena, Montana, he currently resides in Gig Harbor, Washington.

You can connect with me on:
- https://www.djquinnauthor.com

Made in the USA
Columbia, SC
24 June 2024

a04db30f-d15e-4edb-8df9-1596a8f7abbdR01